The Imus Ranch

Cooking for Kids and Cowboys

Deirdre Imus

RODALE

For Daevin Kirschner

July 23, 1985—March 7, 2002

"A long long time ago I can still remember how that music used to make me smile and I knew if I had my chance that I could make those people dance and maybe they'd be happy for a while . . ."

—from "American Pie" by Don McLean

Printed in the United States of America
Rodale Inc. makes every effort to use acid-free ∞, recycled paper ♻ .

Cover design by Andy Carpenter
Interior design by Dina Dell 'Arciprete/dk Design Partners, Inc.
Photography by Ben Fink

We're always happy to hear from you.
For questions or comments concerning the editorial content of this book,
please write to:
Rodale Inc.
Book Readers' Service
33 East Minor Street
Emmaus, PA 18098

Look for other Rodale books wherever books are sold. Or call us at
(800) 848-4735.

For more information about Rodale and the books and magazines we
publish, visit our World Wide Web site at: **www.rodale.com**

Library of Congress Cataloging-in-Publication Data

Imus, Deirdre.
    The Imus Ranch : cooking for kids and cowboys / by Deirdre Imus.
        p.   cm.
    Includes index.
    ISBN-13 978-0-87596-919-4 hardcover
    ISBN-10 0-87596-919-4 hardcover
    ISBN-13 978-1-59486-226-7 paperback
    ISBN-10 1-59486-226-5 paperback
    1. Vegetarian cookery.   2. Imus Ranch.   I. Title.
TX837.I49   2004
641.5'636—dc22   2003025404

Distributed to the trade by Holtzbrinck Publishers

      4   6   8   10   9   7   5   hardcover
  2   4   6   8   10   9   7   5   3   1   paperback

ACKNOWLEDGMENTS

I'd like to thank my editor, Margot Schupf, and everyone else at Rodale, especially Nancy N. Bailey, Donna Bellis, JoAnn Brader, Patricia Field, and Webster Williams.

David Von Drehle wrote the original essays for "It's All about the Kitchen" and "A Day at the Ranch." He did a terrific job and was fun to work with. Then Charles McCord rewrote "It's All about the Kitchen" and made it genuinely hilarious. He also edited and rewrote "A Day at the Ranch" so that, in Charles' view, you could make sense of it. I think he was kidding.

Ben Fink shot some great photographs. (The cowboys on the ranch loved Ben and Ben loved them.) Dina Dell 'Arciprete Houser did inspired work in the design. Thank you as well to Judith Kern for her recipe writing and to food stylists Stevie Bass and Kim Loughlin.

As we wrote in the opening essay, we've had a number of people work in our kitchen, among them Adrienne Hertz and Elizabeth Ryan. We thank them for their work. There were others who contributed to this book and I hope they all feel a sense of pride in participating in a project where 100 percent of the revenues will help change the lives of these kids with cancer.

I love my agent Esther Newberg. However, no one who deals with her feels as I do, which is *why* I love her.

I owe the biggest thanks to my irascible but most incredible husband.

The kids at the Ranch who agreed to be photographed were wonderful as were the folks who work at the Imus Ranch: Perry, Donnie, Yunk, Matthew, Chicken Jack, Tracy, Andy, Edward, Butch, Sam, Janeene, Tim, Eddie, Frances, Angie, Vicki, Consuelo, Tyler, Jessica, and Bill.

Thank you, everyone.

CONTENTS

WAY BACK WHEN, THERE WAS AN OLD-WEST AXIOM THAT WENT, "IF YOU'RE GOING TO OPERATE A SUCCESSFUL WORKING CATTLE RANCH, DON'T TRY TO DO IT WITHOUT GOOD HORSES AND A GOOD COOK." THEY'RE ABSOLUTE, BEDROCK FUNDAMENTALS.

Might as well try to run a bank without green eyeshades and money. On the Imus Ranch, even when the kids and cowhands are tied up doing any of a thousand different chores, the kitchen's still in the back of their minds. No, make that the *front.* So, when we lose a cook, we could just as well lose a limb. It happens, though, and when it does, the place goes into a full-tilt, Custer's Last Stand, we're-all-gonna-die panic.

Unfortunately, not only does it happen, but it also happens a lot. There are more good horses, we've learned, than good cooks. Or, at least, horses that aren't, you know, paging themselves over the intercom.

Cooks are nuts. No, that's too abrasive. Cooks are . . . artists. That's better. I have never met a touchier, more temperamental species in my life. Their idiosyncrasies are in an unending struggle with their *issues.* Like the chef we started out with five years ago: a luridly flamboyant Eastern European woman from Albuquerque, New Mexico, who designed and, I suspect, occasionally cooked handbags when she wasn't chasing children around the kitchen with her fingers spread antlerlike atop her head, hollering, "Chocolate mousse! Chocolate mousse!" It didn't help that she tended to engage in the Mousse Act at around 5:30 in the

late afternoon, with hungry kids and cowboys due in at 6:00 P.M. to eat. I remember her nodding solemnly as I tried to explain the Ranch's philosophy of healthy living and healthy cooking, as well as our schedule, and that we would find it agreeable if she could use that 5:30 to 6:00 window of time for food preparation rather than animal emulation. Apparently, not all of it sank in.

One day, another member of the staff had some business to tend to in Ms. Mousse's bunkhouse, and she happened to open the refrigerator. I won't say the staffer fainted, but she did come to me in a dead run, aghast, saying, "You're not going to believe this, but the Mousse has a stash of bleached flour and white sugar in there!" We subsequently found that Mousse had similar toxic stuff stashed *everywhere.* In fact, I wondered why she didn't have a squirrel act, given the amount of health-jeopardizing junk she'd secretly stockpiled all over the ranch. Though it left us temporarily chef-less, we *did* exercise our termination option.

As fortune would have it, the Ranch gardener abruptly announced at that point that *he* was a chef. Who knew? Well, fine, just so long as he didn't try to use a spade as a spatula, or whatever. We had high expectations until we discovered that he and the sous chef (a person *he* recommended) hated each other. Which brought to mind another axiom: "When the chef and his assistant are continually trying to skewer each other with rotisserie spits, kitchen efficiency may be compromised." Besides, blood on the floor seemed inconsistent with our strict vegan philosophy. We told them good-bye.

For a while we employed a sour, hostile, embittered, horrible woman who said she had run a vegetarian restaurant in Santa Fe. Hey, she said she could cook. Our spirits and optimism soared. Until we discovered that her restaurant hadn't done all that well. In fact, what it *had* done was bomb. How in the world you manage to take down a vegetarian restaurant in yuppie-infested Santa Fe is beyond me. It's like tanking with a steakhouse in Fort Worth, Texas. And she hated kids—strike two. We hated her—strike three.

Our next kitchen crew was notable mainly for their tattoos. And nose rings. And do-rags and hip-hop shorts. I can't recall exactly where they came from. Leavenworth? Folsom? But watching them slicing and dicing in our beautiful Ranch kitchen had a sort of surreal, Truman Capote, *In Cold Blood* quality. Kind of like a squad of Hell's Angels had scored a gig on the Food Network. After they had prepared a meal, the kitchen always seemed to look as though a train had derailed in the place, with great loss of life. Annoying. And their cooking was not great. But who was going to tell them? It finally fell to my husband to ask one of them to resign after a pay period unaccountably sought 8,546 hours of overtime for a particular individual. They *all* quit—which became clear to us when we walked in for lunch one afternoon and found the kitchen strewn with chef's pants, aprons, and smocks . . . and no staff. Actually, we felt a sense of relief. At least they hadn't killed us.

Every time we change chefs, the drama and the trauma are extreme. All hands, kids included, start buzzing and worrying, "Are we going to starve?" You learn once again that *it really is all about*

the kitchen! Literally. The Ranch can't function without it, which is why I have to say, thank goodness for extraordinary means of life support. In this case, that's Tim Buckley, our paramedic and always the guy who rescues us. Somehow, somewhere, Tim learned to cook. And cook well. If the food preparation staff goes down, there's Tim. After our Hell's Angel emergency, Tim stepped in and managed to get breakfast on the table every day for a month. If he ever gets some anger-management therapy, he could be great. Tim has issues. But then, all cooks have issues.

On that terrible day—the day when the Crips and Bloods stiffed us—we all gathered up at the horse barn, trying to decide what to do. Thirty people, many of them kids, famished—and the kitchen was like Al Capone's safe. Tim, bless 'im, volunteered as always. Then other people stepped forward saying, "I can cook this" or "I can make that." It was nuts. It was also a re-

minder: When there's nothing cooking in the kitchen, it affects everything else on the Ranch. I'm sure the same is true in your home: There's just something about the kitchen. You know how friends and guests always seem to gravitate to that one, inviting space—the most friendly and reassuring room in the whole house? And, if I have my way, it's the healthiest as well.

In this book, I've tried to share the warmth and the philosophy of the Imus Ranch, which is constructed on the idea of healthy living. As you'll see, we have integrated that idea into every aspect of our lives. It starts with what we put into our bodies. And the center of it all is the kitchen.

A DAY AT THE RANCH

ids come from all over to the Imus Ranch. Some are cancer survivors. Some are still battling cancer. Some have life-threatening blood disorders, and some have lost a brother or sister to sudden infant death syndrome. You might imagine there would be a lot of sadness here, but there isn't. We welcome kids who have known too much sickness and too much death, and we give them something they urgently need: a sense of independence and purpose through healthy, vigorous living.

The Imus Ranch is about work, in large doses. It's about self-reliance, self-discipline, and inner strength. It's about getting free of toxins—chemical toxins and mental toxins—that poison our bodies and minds. On the Imus Ranch, we use no pesticides, no chemical fertilizers, no toxic cleaning agents. Every structure was built, foundation to rooftop, with environmentally friendly materials and finished with nontoxic paints. Much of the organic food we eat is grown right in our own greenhouse. The Imus Ranch is not just a place; it is a mind-set and a way of life. Through this book, I want to share the Ranch and our philosophy with you.

Every year, more and more people are becoming aware of the dangers posed by toxins that contaminate our environment and threaten us. When I was in high school and first began paying attention to what I was putting into my body, there was no such thing as a natural-foods supermarket. You had to hunt down small specialty shops if you wanted to buy organic. That's changed. Americans now spend some $8 billion annually on organic foods, an amount that's growing by about 20 percent a year. Half of all organic foods are now sold in conventional supermarkets—up from just 7 percent in 1995. Still, as you see all we're doing to live a truly nontoxic life at the Imus Ranch, you might say, "It's overwhelming. I can't do all this!"

You can. *Start simply, with just one or two things.*

You'd be surprised how much you can accomplish by trying. Let me tell you a story.

A girl named Audie, a cancer patient, visited the Ranch. We treat all the kids here exactly alike—as normal kids, not fragile china dolls. No one on our staff ever mentions disease. Audie had been off chemotherapy only for a few months, and she was afraid to get on a horse. "What if I fall off or hit my head and my cancer comes back?" she asked me.

I kept pushing her to try.

"You're so mean!" she shouted. "I hate you, I hate you!"

Finally, Audie did get on her horse, though all the time she was telling me how horrible I was. Two days later, she gave me a huge hug. She couldn't stop thanking me. *She was riding!* She had conquered her fear and *herself* and couldn't be more proud of what she had accomplished. Audie was having fun, living. As she said: "It was the best thing that ever happened to me."

Kids arrive at the Imus Ranch in the afternoon, 10 in each group, all between the ages of 11 and 16. For some, it's their first trip away from parents and home, and perhaps their first time on an airplane. They pair up with roommates and begin looking around the hacienda, the main house where Don and Wyatt and I live. Not long after they get here, we all have our first dinner together—on this particular night, it's a gorgeous leafy salad, broccoli soup, and veggie lasagna. Afterward, Don and I gather the kids and explain a few rules:

"Don't leave your junk lying around."

And "Don't yell."

And "Don't slam doors."

We tell them to drink a lot of water and use plenty of sunblock.

Oh, and "Never leave your hat on your bed," we caution them. "Bad luck!"

The kids are sitting on overstuffed cushions in the Great Room. Don and I are in chairs with the sun setting in the big windows behind us. Country music drifts in from the stereo system in the dining room next door. It's Waylon Jennings. There's nothing even remotely in-stitutional about this place.

Don adds a warning: "Whenever you're around horses, you have to be careful," he says. "These aren't Camp Happy Face horses. These are real cowboy horses."

The kids are anxious to get down the hill to the Old West town we've built called Reader's Digest, New Mexico, in honor of one of our most generous supporters. But before we can leave, there's one more rule to discuss: "If you don't wash your feet at night," Don says, "the coyotes will sneak in and suck your toes while you sleep." There's a pause, then everyone laughs, and the kids all pile into the back of a pickup truck for the quarter-mile ride to town.

Inside the Unilever General Store, the kids take their first step toward becoming cowboys and cowgirls. The racks and tables are piled high with Wrangler jeans and western shirts, Justin boots, Resistol hats, belts, and big rodeo-style buckles. They dive into the merchandise—it's all donated by Ranch patrons—and race one another to the fitting rooms. There's Julie, a shy girl with blond hair. She goes into the fitting room as a typical American teenager and comes back out ready for the range. Between the tomato red shirt with cowboy piping and the brim of her white straw hat, Julie wears a big grin that shows her braces.

Some kids punch the keys of the antique cash register on the counter; others plunge their hands into the gum-ball jar. From the woodstove in the center of the room to the creaking wooden porch to the wood ceiling finished to resemble the ceiling that the writer D. H. Lawrence painted at Mabel Dodge Luhan's house in Taos, every detail of the place is designed to take the kids back in time. We've also tried to anticipate every need they may have: Behind the counter are disposable cameras donated by Fuji, Oral-B toothbrushes, and an array of toiletries—shaving cream, sunblock, and deodorant—including JR Liggett soaps, which are free of synthetic chemicals.

Everything goes into big cloth laundry bags. Some of the younger kids wobble under the weight of everything as they haul their gear back to the truck. A few are a little on the bashful side at first; others are animated and boisterous. Two boys, Josh and Harlan, scamper after a rabbit that just disappeared beneath the porch. Wyatt grabs the new hat of a pigtailed girl named Mariah and runs off with it, giggling. A hummingbird hovers over a big planter of flowers and then flits away.

The kids end the evening across the dusty road at the Bull and Bear Dance Hall—sponsored by the New York Stock Exchange—where they hit the pool table, the poker table, and the pinball machines. Of course, country music's on the huge jukebox. It's Delbert McClinton. But there's not much time for cards and eight-ball tonight. Bedtime's 9 P.M. sharp. Days start early on a working cattle spread.

The Imus Ranch is 4,000 unspoiled acres set in rolling hills and mesa country about 50 miles east of Santa Fe, New Mexico. Our front gate is about 6,000 feet above sea level and right on the old Santa Fe Trail. In a way, you can get a feeling for the whole history of the settling of the West from the Ranch's entrance because the ruts of the famous old wagon trail actually are still visible in spots. Now, not far away, an Amtrak main line runs across a section of the Ranch. And just a short distance from the railroad, there's an interstate that tracks that same timeworn route between the peaks of the Sangre de Cristo Mountains to the north and the Sandia range to the south. Scattered brush, grass, and wildflowers give the landscape a quilted look—a pleasing patchwork of sandy browns and mottled greens as seen by travelers flying over this part of northern New Mexico.

This is a dry part of the world, which gives the air lightness on even the hottest days. Still, most afternoons in summer, thunderheads pile up over the Sangre de Cristo and make their way toward us. Usually, the rain is all spilled by the time the clouds reach the Ranch, but sometimes they burst right over us. With thunder booming and lightning snapping, the rain pours off the stony soil and races downhill along deeply etched arroyo streambeds. These sudden washes dry up as quickly as they arrive, leaving behind gullies and furrows in the red clay and sandstone. Coyotes use the arroyos as hidden passageways to conceal their travels across the landscape.

I loved this land from the moment I first saw it. It was one of the most beautiful places I'd ever been. After Don and I met in 1991, we began traveling through the Southwest in our free time, and because I had grown up in Connecticut and gone to school in Pennsylvania, the sheer dimensions of this vast, open country were amazing to me. But I felt immediately at peace here. We were married in Monument Valley, the breathtaking backdrop of so many John Ford Westerns. On one of our trips, we visited the ranch in northern Arizona where Don grew up, a place named the Willows. It's all public land now, but the house where Don lived as a boy is still there, shaded by willow trees. A stone hanging in the kitchen was carved simply: 1884 WILLIAM IMUS. Don talked about how the happiest days of his life had been spent on that ranch, doing chores, riding horses, herding cattle. It was hard work, but that's what made it worthwhile.

While all this was going on, more and more of our time was spent thinking about children and their health. Before we met, Don began hosting an annual radiothon to benefit the

Tomorrows Children's Fund and the CJ Foundation for SIDS charities. Over the years, he raised enough money to build the Don Imus WFAN Pediatric Center for Tomorrows Children, a seven-story treatment and research facility that's part of the Hackensack University Medical Center, the country's sixth largest hospital complex located just outside New York City in Hackensack, New Jersey. After Don invited me to help out with the project in 1992, the radiothon became a part of my life, too. For the first time, I saw how many children are being diagnosed with cancer and life-threatening blood diseases. I found myself thinking: These kids should not be getting sick in the *first* place. The fact is, a high percentage of all known cancers are environmentally linked. Kids are exposed to pesticides and other toxic substances both inside and outside the home. Toxins are everywhere. They're in pest-control products for our homes. They're in pest-control products for our pets. They're in everyday household supplies, from the cleaning closet to the medicine chest, and even in our food. Children are the most vulnerable to these chemicals—especially indoors where enclosed spaces concentrate the toxic effects. Children breathe faster than adults, and their cells turn over faster, too. As a result, kids absorb contaminants faster.

We felt we had to do something about it.

These two ideas, the great American West and a healthier way of raising children, began to come together for us in early 1998 after we'd visited the old Imus family ranch in Arizona. We had completed another successful radiothon, but we wanted to do more. I remember the day it took form: Don was in his office preparing for an interview. I was pregnant with Wyatt and working out on a treadmill. Suddenly, Don burst in, yelling, "I've got it!"

If you know Don, you know he's not the type to get terribly worked up over things. The guy heard by millions each morning—that laconic cowboy with the gruff voice and vicious wit—that's real. That's Don. So when he came rushing in, genuinely excited, he got my attention.

The memory of his childhood and the needs of children struggling with illness and grief had come together in an amazing idea: We could create a wonderful retreat: a working cattle ranch where such kids could live and work alongside real cowboys and discover a more nourishing, richer lifestyle. The idea was perfect.

Eagerly, we began firing suggestions back and forth. To a remarkable degree, the Ranch we envisioned that day is the Ranch that was built. When I imagined the hacienda, I pictured something like the Ponderosa on the old *Bonanza* television series—a big house with a warm, family feeling. The vision of an authentic Old West town was also there from the beginning. We

would build a dance hall filled with games and art supplies and have bunkhouses for staff and guests. Don had the idea of making the infirmary into a saloon where kids could belly up to the bar to take their medicines. We would have fully equipped hospital rooms, in case we ever need them—but they would be decorated in the style of an 1880s bordello. The office would be located inside a marshal's office fit for Wyatt Earp, with desks and phones in the jail cells.

We also knew that the Ranch would be nontoxic and biodynamic, meaning that our farming techniques would work not just to exploit the earth, but also to restore and sustain the earth. Everything we did—from the way we constructed roads and buildings to the way we furnished the Ranch to how we grew our crops and prepared our food—would be environmentally friendly and health-promoting. The purpose was not just to entertain the Ranch kids but also to open their eyes to a healthy way of living: clean, green, and completely organic.

I can't say it too often: This is not a play camp. Don and I are convinced that work and responsibility build confidence, self-esteem, and self-worth. Remember, a lot of these kids have been diagnosed with cancer. Their doctors and parents put limitations on them, understandably. We don't do that. The purpose here is for these kids to work hard, to learn to ride a horse, and to care for the animals—to take responsibility and recover their self-sufficiency.

Long before sunup, Don goes to work in his state-of-the-art studio adjacent to the dance hall. Millions of people listen to his broadcasts from Reader's Digest (population: 7; elevation: 6,264 feet). High-speed phone lines and satellite technology allow Don to work from the Ranch as if he were back East at WFAN. A 100-year-old Navajo blanket hangs on the wall as a backdrop for the MSNBC cameras, and the wooden floor (required for proper acoustics) is hand-painted to look like terra-cotta tile.

While Don broadcasts, the ranch hands start getting ready for work. By 5:30 A.M. our kitchen staff is preparing breakfast. Two child-life specialists from the Tomorrows Children's Fund at Hackensack University Medical Center, who travel out each time a group of kids is here, rouse the kids. Around 6 A.M., the sun bursts from behind the hills and rises above the AT&T Horse Barn, even as the moon still lingers over a distant mesa to the west.

Donnie Imus, our nephew, meets the kids in the big red barn. He's the head wrangler. Yesterday, these kids were teens and preteens in shorts and T-shirts; this morning, they are cowboys and cowgirls in their jeans and boots and long-sleeved shirts. Each child has been assigned a horse to ride—like Big John or Molly or Linus or Cinnamon; Bonnie, Woody, or P.J. Some of the kids are a little sleepy-eyed. Mariah complains good-naturedly that two of the boys kept her up all night, talking. But the boys don't seem much the worse for it: They're as playful and spunky as they were the night before. When Josh notices one of our cowboys, named Yunk, twirling a lariat, he asks, "Can you rope good?"

"Fair," Yunk answers. For a cowboy, that's a speech. For Yunk, that's an epic.

"Can you rope me if I'm running?" And off Josh goes, with Yunk chasing him, spurs jingling. A few steps later, Josh's leg is in a noose.

The kids listen intently as Donnie explains the ritual of feeding the horses. After a few minutes of instruction—just that quickly—the work begins. Donnie and the kids work from stall to stall, dropping fresh green hay into the feed bins with a scoop of a mixture of grains and some garlic for improved circulation and to keep flies, mosquitoes, and other pests away. Then the kids climb into the back of a pickup to feed the horses out in the pasture.

"*Baaaaaa* to you, too!" Mariah shouts as the truck bounces past the sheep barn.

After early chores, breakfast is served in the hacienda dining room, where we have three long tables set with thick, unmatched earthenware plates. Many people imagine that a healthy diet must be strange and alien, but the breakfast laid out on the sturdy antique servers would be familiar in just about any home. The chefs have prepared scrambled eggs and waffles; there are also fresh fruit, cereals, and soy sausages. There are pitchers of springwater and juice on each table and Imus Ranch salsa for the eggs.

The kids need to eat a big meal because they have a lot to do for the rest of the day. For example, the stalls must be cleaned. Matthew, another cowboy, gives directions. Four of the girls, armed with brooms and shovels, can't believe what they're about to do, but they gamely begin sweeping the day-old straw, sand, and dust from the stall floors. The boys grab rakes to load the horse dung into carts.

Raking and shoveling alongside them is Howard A. Pearson, M.D., professor emeritus of pediatric hematology at Yale University. Dr. Pearson is a legend among America's pediatric specialists—a former president of the American Academy of Pediatrics and the driving force behind Paul Newman's Hole in the Wall Gang Camp for kids with cancer. We call Dr. Pearson the most overeducated man in America because he has degrees from Dartmouth, Harvard, and Yale. To the kids, however, he's just a friend in a T-shirt, helping to muck out the stalls.

Donnie Imus is the head wrangler at the Ranch. Here he's showing the kids how to hold and twirl a rope. The ultimate goal is to perform this task from the back of a horse chasing a calf who's running about 30 miles an hour.

Notice the glove on Donnie's right hand? Don't ask. He's about to hand the rope to one of the kids who will

attempt to rope a bucket. Next he'll rope a plastic steer head stuck in a bale of hay. By the time this kid leaves

the Ranch, he'll be roping Donnie!

"Good upper-body exercise!" the doctor says cheerfully. "Plus, it gives me a chance to see the kids first thing in the morning." Without their knowing it, the kids are being monitored by one of the most distinguished physicians in the country.

It's 8 A.M. The sun's climbing higher in a faint blue sky. Guinea hens are honking in the juniper scrub. A rooster crows in the chicken yard. This is going to be a hot one.

When we found this property, we knew immediately that it was perfect. It's hard to say *how* we knew. The land was completely undeveloped—we would put in water, roads, electricity. The pastures were choked with juniper and locoweed—acres and acres of the stuff—that would all have to be cleared before we could run cattle. There wasn't a well or a wire on the whole parcel. Still, we looked at it and somehow saw what it could become. We committed to the dream. We bought the first 810 acres without knowing whether anyone would buy into the idea. But we jumped in, all the time asking ourselves: "What if this is just crazy? What if we can't raise any money?"

Don went on the radio to see whether his audience would join in the vision. The response was unbelievable—and reassuring. He raised $4 million in the first three hours! Hundreds of individuals, families, and companies gave generously, many of them "buying" an acre of the Ranch for $5,000. The names of all these initial donors are engraved on large, floor-to-ceiling limestone tablets on either side of the entry foyer in the hacienda. It's impressive and a heartfelt thank-you. Many other donors' names are painted in prominent locations around the Ranch. The largest donors have facilities named in their honor, like the Joseph Abboud Family Riding Arena, the AFLAC Rodeo Arena, the AFLAC Hay Barn, and the AT&T Horse Barn. Hackensack University Medical Center sponsored the infirmary, which we named the Black Lamb Saloon in honor of the first lamb born on the Ranch. Other major corporate supporters include Fuji, American Express, General Motors, Ford, Daimler/Chrysler Jeep, NASDAQ, Nikon, the Ward Family/SLI, General Electric, Gillette, Unilever, Justin Boots, Wrangler, Resistol, and a couple anonymous donors who each contributed well over a million dollars.

People just seemed to get the concept right from the start: this vision of kids actually living and *working* on a cattle ranch, soaking up the not-quite-lost virtues of the Old West.

A big part of the objective here is that we are able to live with these kids as one big family. It all goes back to Don and his memories of where he grew up among the ranch hands and his mom and dad. They were such great times for him, and he wanted to share that kind of experience—as closely as possible—with these kids.

⚜

A magnificent mesa looms over the Imus Ranch. The flat summit is more than 7,000 feet above sea level and 2 miles from one end to the other. We like to drive the kids up there to hike, hunt for arrowheads, play games, and just fool around. The mesa is so massive that it makes even the 14,000-square-foot hacienda look small and cozy by comparison. People are surprised to step inside the main house and find such large, open, and *healing* spaces.

An important part of the holistic concept of the Ranch is that the buildings are made from environmentally friendly materials. The hacienda, for example, is made entirely of straw bales mortared with adobe. All the wood is recycled or reclaimed: No pressure-treated wood, with its inherent toxicity, was used anywhere on the Ranch. All our paint finishes are nontoxic—Benjamin Moore has a line of safe, water-based paints and generously donated a huge selection of colors. I was able to find an especially patient plasterer who wasn't driven to distraction by my desire to create my own colors for the hacienda rooms. He mixed the shades using milk and lime—an old-fashioned method that is totally nontoxic—and remixed them, and remixed them again, until what I saw on the walls matched what I saw in my mind.

And I'm not afraid of color. Quite the opposite. In fact, you might say I'm color-aggressive. But I had a clear idea of what I wanted. Kids visiting the Ranch would live with us in the hacienda, two to a room, and while the rooms would have similarities, I wanted each to be unique: A different color on every wall, but all would have a calming sky blue ceiling in common. I stayed away from bright hues, instead choosing warm, rich, elegant tones for a soothing, more meditative environment. Colors can actually enhance healing. Everyone who comes

EDUCATE YOURSELF

DID YOU KNOW THAT . . .

Lead is still a serious health hazard. Although the use of lead in house paint has been illegal for more than 30 years, it is still found in older buildings and is still in many plumbing systems. To reduce the amount of lead in your drinking water, let the water run for 30 to 60 seconds before using it. That initial flow will eliminate most heavy metals, including lead, that may have collected in the pipes.

here notices it. They say, "The colors are amazing!" They're simply experiencing the positive response, or reaction, that color itself can produce.

All the bathroom sinks we used have the same hand-painted porcelain, but each sink is done differently, finished with the image of an animal. We have at least one antique piece of furniture in every bedroom. I created an original painting for every room to hang between the twin beds. Don "auctioned" them on the air and was able to raise $25,000 for the Ranch—we honor those contributors with nameplates on each of the paintings. I've tried to give this same attention to detail to the design of every room in the house.

We built the hacienda in a horseshoe shape enclosing a courtyard in which the central element is a big, soothing fountain. Don and I and Wyatt have our bedrooms at the southwest corner of the horseshoe, which is in balance with our traditional Chinese feng shui environmental requirements. The center of the house is the Great Room, with an ebony Steinway grand piano, soft chairs, a chess board (many of the kids play the game), and a big, curving window seat, large enough for several kids to curl up on in the warm sun. Next to the Great Room is the dining room, which easily holds 30 people for a meal without feeling like a dormitory cafeteria or a mess hall. Even though it's large, the dining room is also warm, rustic, handsome, and inviting. It has a big, friendly opening into a copious kitchen, which adds to the homey feeling of the whole place. In fact, much of the traffic in and out of the house during the day passes right through the kitchen, where there's always a Thermos of Gatorade, a cooler of filtered springwater, a plate of fruit, a jar of raw organic mixed nuts, a basket of Luna Bars, and organic chocolates for hungry and thirsty cowboys. People coming and going throughout the day can watch the big meals progressing, from idea to preparation to presentation. Sometimes, kids see herbs and vegetables they have harvested from the greenhouse transformed into delicious servings on their plates that very same evening. For many, it's the first time they've experienced the connection between the food they put in their mouths and the earth and plants all around them. They realize that food *comes* from somewhere—somewhere besides a supermarket shelf or a fast-food joint—and that it matters how that food is produced and grown.

We divide the kids into two groups on their first day here. One group does chores—feeding the cattle and the buffalo, checking the water in the troughs, surveying fences, weeding gardens, harvesting in the greenhouse—while the other group learns the basics of handling a horse. In the afternoon, they switch.

I'd never been on a horse until we bought the Ranch. Don insisted that I learn to ride. Twice he had seen me run the New York City Marathon, and he had watched me compete in triathlons. So he knew I had the physical skills to do it. "Just get on the horse and ride," he said. I climbed onto a palomino and went galloping off. I was scared out of my pants. I was crying. For days, I did little more than scream and hang on. But, little by little, I started to get the hang of it and even advanced.

As the kids spend their first day with the horses learning, step-by-step, to work them, they get fundamental instruction not only in learning to ride but also in the responsibility of feeding and grooming the animals. As Don said that first night, these aren't docile dude-ranch horses. They're well-trained quarter horses, cowboy horses in every sense of the phrase.

So, around 9 A.M., Yunk gathers the kids around Rockin' Doc's stall. We call him Rocker for short—a beautiful bay quarter horse that I bought for Don after he was violently thrown and almost killed in a freak riding accident at the Ranch. With time, we have come to think of Rocker as my horse and an animal named King as Don's horse. Still, Don looks terrific riding Rocker. That horse is truly splendid. In fact, if you ask him nicely, he'll even kneel down to help you climb aboard.

Horse training starts a little late today. Woody, normally a sturdy animal, went lame without warning this morning. His entire left forequarter seized up. The injury was a mystery to Donnie and Yunk. They studied and massaged the rippling breast muscle. Then Donnie gave his limping horse a long shower with the hose. But nothing seemed to make much difference. Donnie has called Dr. Michael Callahan, the veterinarian, and while we wait for him to arrive, Yunk uses the time to give the kids some more elements of primary horse handling.

There are so many things to know: How to lay the lead rope over a horse's neck before slipping it around the nose. How to step from the stall ahead of your horse. How to tie a quick-release knot to hold your horse while you brush the coat and clean the shoes. After we brush Imus Ranch horses, we spray them with a microbial solution called Kritter Spritz. It breaks down the bacteria that attract flies, but it's also so completely nontoxic that a person can drink the stuff. Donnie likes to squirt some in his mouth to show how safe it is. We also buy an organic shampoo to use when we wash the horses. It cleans better than the chemical stuff. "You look at the horse and say, I didn't know he was *that* color," says Don.

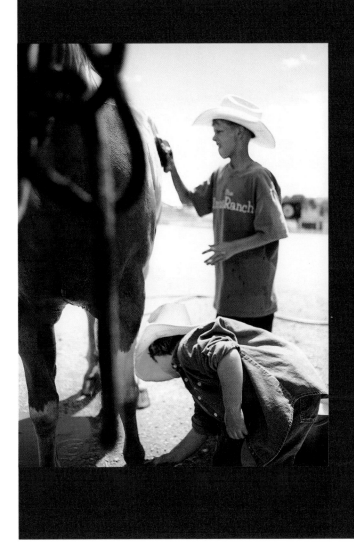

EDUCATE
YOURSELF

By 9:30, the sky is azure and the air is getting hot. Yunk's introduction to horsemanship must be one of the longest speeches in cowboy history. He's an excellent teacher. Part of that is *what* he has to say: the careful, item-by-item explanation of how to meet a horse, gain its confidence, and prepare it for a ride. Part of it is *how* he says things: slowly, softly, simply. Part of it is how he *looks* while he says things: Yunk is a classic cowboy, lean as a branding iron—all sinew and joints—with a belt buckle as big as a saucer.

By the time he finishes talking half an hour later, the kids know enough to groom, bridle, and saddle their horses, and they're itching to ride. But we start them instead with a mile-long walk, leading their horses down through the Old West town and back up the hill past the

sheep pen. It's important that they get comfortable with the horses and the horses grow accustomed to taking their lead from these kids.

As the group is preparing to walk, Doc Callahan comes driving up the road, a plume of dust rising behind his truck. Everything pauses so that the kids can watch the veterinarian work; their schedules have to be flexible so that they can have the real experience of a rancher. After a brief examination, Doc Callahan arrives at a theory: A year earlier, Woody was out in the pasture, and when we found him the next morning, his lower leg was bleeding profusely from a deep gash. Who knows what happened? No one expected him to make it, but somehow Woody healed so well that he actually wound up better than before. Doc Callahan surmises that after all this time, an infection has suddenly set in, blocking proper circulation of blood to the leg.

I ask Donnie whether Woody has been eating his garlic. He has, Donnie answers. As the kids watch intently, Doc Callahan gives Woody a dose of antibiotics.

Afterward, the kids put bridles on their horses and we all set off walking past a still pond in the rising heat. Dragonflies buzz and hover just above the surface; a rooster crows; a sheep bleats. A light breeze faintly, thankfully, rustles the leaves on our new fruit trees. Don leads the way, riding Rocker.

🌿

Meanwhile, the other half of our group is off doing chores with Chicken Jack and Tracy, a generous, friendly couple who were living in New Mexico and listening to Don's show when he started talking about our vision for the Ranch. Jack and Tracy were hooked immediately and wanted to help out to shut him up. They started meeting our flights at the Santa Fe airport carrying signs: WILL WORK FOR FOOD. How could we *not* bring them on? Chicken Jack is a great ranch hand—a jack-of-all-trades who can feed cattle one minute and change oil the next. More important, he is awesome with the kids. Jack's wife, Tracy, has an unbelievable green thumb. She's managed to get our organic gardening program up and working—and that's not easy. Tracy coaxes amazing plants to grow and flourish. Walking into her greenhouse is like stepping into a cartoon world of superplants and megaveggies.

Josh and Julie head off with Tracy to water the flowers in town and weed the vegetable patch. Then, after tending to the tomatoes, cucumbers, and zucchini, the kids go to the greenhouse to gather some produce. Josh and Julie discover leafy vegetables growing with such

EDUCATE
YOURSELF

exuberance that the beds seem too small to hold them. They marvel at the tight clusters of lacinto and leafy green kale, the robust collard greens, the white-stemmed bok choy, the purple leaves signaling buried beets, and tough green leaves indicating succulent leeks. And most amazing, the deep dark green chard—called rainbow Swiss chard because of the astonishing colors of the stalks: blood orange, neon yellow, hot pink. Herbs grow on the greenhouse tables: rosemary, oregano, sage, peppermint, and some of the biggest basil you've ever seen. Tracy babies these plants along, helping them to thrive in a nontoxic environment. Instead of using chemical fertilizers and pesticides and herbicides, we make our own compost and use pure organic treatments. The only pest visible in the greenhouse (other than my husband) is the tiny, whining white fly (wait a minute, that *is* my husband) that Tracy wards off with oil from the Indian neem tree and garlic juice.

Josh and Julie take scissors and begin snipping leaves of chard for the larder. In minutes, they have a heaping basketful. Tracy washes the leaves in a sink, and the kids cooperate to stuff the chard into nontoxic Evert-Fresh bags. (I've learned that standard plastic bags and aluminum foil, in fact, have toxic properties. After some searching, I managed to find this alternative that is not only environmentally friendly but also performs better.) Evert-Fresh bags keep greens fresh for weeks. And it's a good thing the bags preserve so well because without even trying, the kids have harvested pounds and pounds of chard. When they are done stuffing three bulging bags, the kids carry their harvest up to the hacienda kitchen and pack the bags into our refrigerated pantry.

While Julie, Josh, and Tracy are working, the rest of the morning chore crew load up in Chicken Jack's truck and set off to find the cattle herd. We have about 40 head of Texas longhorn cattle on the Ranch. Our bull is named River Wide; he was one of the top longhorns in the nation when we bought him. He lives with about a dozen cows and their calves in one section of pasture. River Wide and his posse amble along and graze happily. Both male and female boast those ultrawide sets of horns that seem to symbolize the Old West. The herd is never far from the five donkeys that share their pastures and that are always on the alert for possible predators. I'll bet you didn't know it, but donkeys make great watchdogs! Our steers graze separately because the last thing we need is one of them getting into a fight with River Wide.

By the time the kids are ready to leave the Ranch, some of them will actually be riding well enough to help us herd cattle from one pasture to another. That's genuine cowboy stuff. Even the kids who don't ride as well like to watch whenever the ranch hands use their skilled and crafty quarter horses to move the herd or to cut young bulls from the rest of the animals to be neutered into steers.

A vegan cattle ranch is sort of a contradiction in terms, I suppose. I like to think of the cattle as moving pieces of architecture, not beef on the hoof. Our animals graze for the sake of grazing—not to prepare them for some gruesome slaughterhouse.

Wide-open country with ample forage, plenty of company, nothing but time and pasture stretching before them: This is truly longhorn heaven.

🌿

Jack's hand has a couple of angry gouges that he got when he broke up a fight between a dog and a cat. People keep asking whether he is all right, but he brushes the question aside. "I just have to cowboy up, " he says, cleaning his hand. It's one of the key concepts of Western life and an idea we live by on the Imus Ranch. I'd explain it this way: When you're ignoring pain, brushing past hardship, doing your best despite adversity—that's when you know what it means to "cowboy up."

It's a precept I can relate to. As an athlete, I used similar terms to express the idea that success sometimes requires some suffering and some grit. But whether you say "suck it up" or "cowboy up," the idea is the same: Nothing worth having comes without hard work and sacrifice.

I grew up in Connecticut. My mother was an opera singer, a mezzo-soprano. Today, she hosts a little radio show. My father has his own financial consulting firm. For as long as I can remember, I loved to run. I used to run all the way to school each morning. But once I got to school, they had nothing athletic for the girls to do. Only the boys ran at the annual relay races. So one day, I challenged the fastest boy in school to a race—and I beat him. It was such a great feeling. I remember thinking: *I'm going to the Olympics!*

I enjoyed—and I enjoy to this day—competing with the opposite gender. My high school was a Catholic parochial school with very little for the girls except cheerleading. So I went out for the boys' track team, and I made it. Once I was on the team, I set out to be the fastest. And that's what got me started on living a healthy, nontoxic life: I figured it would make me lean and mean—fitter and stronger and faster than the boys.

I started going to vitamin stores: As I mentioned, there simply weren't any natural-foods supermarkets then. I read all the books I could get my hands on. One was *Dining in the Raw,* by Rita Romano, and I started making all sorts of power shakes and drinks: green-algae shakes, egg-protein shakes, soy-protein shakes. I stopped eating meat. How did I know what to do? I experimented with my own body, trying to figure out what worked. I let my body tell me which foods were building strength and which were detrimental.

I got to be the fastest kid in my school, and Villanova University recruited me to run sprints—the 100-meter and 200-meter races, along with the 300-meter hurdles. That, in particular, is a brutal event: a long sprint with an obstacle every 25 yards or so. I lasted a year on the Villanova team, and in that year I learned that if you want to compete at that level, you have to commit 100 percent. I couldn't dedicate myself totally to athletics, but I never changed my attitude toward my body and my health.

While my diet helped me get strong, it definitely ruined every Thanksgiving in our home. I can still hear myself: "If you guys are going to eat a turkey, it better be organic . . ." "I can't believe these bread crumbs—all bleached out . . ." I was awful. Grandma would say, "Look at me: I'm 72, and I'm eating this turkey. You kids are crazy!"

Over time, however, I learned how to reach people. Lecturing is absolutely the wrong approach. You either make people think you *are* nuts, or you make them mad—or both. That's not the way to get people to change. People change because you provide them with a foundation for making changes—knowledge, backed up by logic—and tell them to start with a few easy things. Those are the keys.

⚜

By 11:30 A.M., the kitchen is busy with preparation of the lunch menu. The chef is adapting a recipe for fusilli pasta with peppers, adding onions for a more intense flavor. Risotto is simmering in a vegan broth. There's a leafy green salad and a rich squash soup. As a treat for Josh and Julie, she's flash-frying some of the chard they picked in the greenhouse. And after lunch, we're having a vegan chocolate birthday cake for one of the kids.

We have an open kitchen with thick, ochre adobe walls and sunlight pouring in through a skylight overhead. A big cooktop, four ovens, plenty of counter space. There are barstools along the counter for people who want to watch the cooks at work or just want to sit and see the traffic pass.

The resources for people who want to eat a healthy diet are so much better now than they were even a few years ago. We grow as much of our own food as we can, and for the rest we have our pick of suppliers. We order provisions from thick catalogs offering thousands of choices: long lists of organic fruits and vegetables, breads, eggs, and soy substitutes for meat and cheese. We order some ingredients from a supplier in Boulder, Colorado, and others from an outfit in Tucson, Arizona. Everything is delivered to the Wild Oats natural-foods store in Santa Fe, and we just cruise down and pick it up. A number of items are available from vendors in the nearby town of Las Vegas, New Mexico.

In other words, the tools for healthy living are out there. My job is to help people find them. And this is where environmentalists sometimes get it wrong. You never have to scare people. You see all these messages out there from environmentalist and Green activists—aggressive, in-your-face messages that exaggerate both the threats and the solutions. They throw it out to frighten everybody but then fail miserably in offering people any realistic, reasonable alternatives.

The Ranch philosophy is to show, in a friendly, welcoming way, that there *are* alternatives. I'm trying to expand this mission beyond the Ranch through the Deirdre Imus Environmental Center for Pediatric Oncology at Hackensack University Medical Center. The idea for the environmental center came to me soon after we began the Ranch project. Kids were coming here who had all been treated in hospitals. And I simply assumed that hospitals would be paramount examples of healthy environments.

But then I began talking with John Ferguson, president of the medical center. He and the institution are huge supporters of the Imus Ranch, so much of what we have accomplished has been with their help. I asked John whether the hospital was using any toxic cleaning agents. Quickly, I discovered that, unwittingly, they were.

I talked about the health risk posed by indoor air pollutants, which have been linked to various forms of cancer, as well as to respiratory illness and a range of allergies. The Environmental Protection Agency did a study of indoor air quality, assessing 20 toxic compounds. Their investigation found that the air we breathe inside is typically *200* times more toxic than

I'm in the "round pen." This is where we warm up our horses, gauge their mood, and get an idea of how sociable they're planning to be. It also gives the kids an opportunity to learn one of the basic fundamentals of horse training. Don calls it "wreck insurance."

The horse is looking at us and he's saying "Please do not make me run around in a circle one more time.

I promise I'll behave. I won't buck. I won't even think about causing a problem. Honest."

the air outdoors. That makes sense when you remember that air outside is constantly circulating, while indoors, toxins are trapped.

I told John that I saw an opportunity to revolutionize the hospital's cleaning program and eliminate all such toxic compounds. After five minutes of my presentation to him, I said, "You could be the first."

He said: "Stop—this makes too much sense. When can we start?"

That was during the winter of 2000. We got a team together and began the task of replacing the toxic-cleaning agents in the hospital with nontoxic cleaning methods that worked every bit as well and often better. I called our operation Greening the Cleaning. It stuck. Almost immediately we won the New Jersey Environmental Quality Award. The citation reads, in part:

> In the spring of 2001, the Deirdre Imus Environmental Center for Pediatric Oncology at Hackensack University Medical Center revamped its massive hospital cleaning operation to reduce not only the toxicity in its cleaning chemicals, but also the quantity of chemicals and waste generated . . . The hospital strives to protect the natural environment as well as to make the hospital safer for patients by reducing the amount of potentially harmful chemicals in the hospital environment.
>
> In a four-phase operation that involved hospital personnel from senior management to the environmental services staff, the hospital replaced 18 of its 22 cleaning products with safer, environmentally sound alternatives that are just as effective. It also began buying cleaning materials in bulk, diluting them at the site to reduce the quantity, and refilling the drums to keep containers out of the waste stream.
>
> The new products are just as effective as the old ones, but without potentially harmful chemicals. For instance, the hospital replaced its existing window cleaner with one that was free from fuming solvents such as ammonia. They also switched to an all-purpose cleaner with no strong acids, chlorine, phosphates, benzene or hazardous ingredients . . . While such changes may seem small, any reduction in hazardous materials will improve indoor air quality and make a big difference to patients who are already in a vulnerable state.

It was a huge deal. Our waste and toxic reduction efforts had cut hospital cleaning costs by 15 percent. The Phillip M. Scanlan Environmental Award came next. Soon, everyone was calling us—companies, hospitals, schools, and businesses in New York, New Jersey, Connecticut, Georgia, Maryland, and Ohio, as well as on Cape Cod and Martha's Vineyard. We're now doing dozens of programs in several hospitals, at Newark Liberty International Airport, at AT&T headquarters, and elsewhere. Our pitch is always the same: Let us offer viable, healthy, nontoxic solutions.

The key is "viable." There are now plenty of nontoxic products that work as well as—or better than—the toxic agents we've grown accustomed to. My whole approach boils down to the idea that green products must be realistic for any mom out there: available, affordable, and realistic. I know from talking to my sister and my friends that most moms are very busy and feel overwhelmed. I don't want to add to anyone's stress load. Most people don't feel they have the time or the energy to read all the books I've read about healthy living. Not only are they not reading the available books, but they're also not reading the labels on the products they buy—and if they *do* read labels, they really don't know what all that stuff means.

EDUCATE YOURSELF

DID YOU KNOW THAT...

The personal care, beauty, and cosmetics industry is among the least regulated of any in this country. Because these products are not sold as drugs, they are not regulated by the Food and Drug Administration, and many contain a wide variety of known toxins and carcinogenic chemicals.

That's just one reason I advocate seeking out natural bath and beauty-care products for the whole family exclusively from companies that are committed to a nontoxic and organic philosophy.

If you're searching for baby products in particular and can't find them at a health food store or pharmacy, log on to one of the following Web sites for more information:

Aubrey Organics at www.aubreyorganics.com; Babyworks catalog at www.babyworks.com; Dr. Hauschka Skin Care at www.drhauschka.com; Jurlique Premium Skincare at www.jurlique.com; Mustela products from France at www.kidstock montana.com/mustela; Natural Family Botanicals at www.nfbotanicals.com/nbcare; Organicbaby information at www.organic baby.com; The Little Forest line at www.naturalbabycareproducts.com

So we need to find ways to make healthy, nontoxic products just as easy to find and as easy to use as all the harmful chemicals in our lives. That's where I'm trying to go with my environmental center. I believe that by bringing awareness of the problem, we raise consciousness—and that brings about change. A demand is created, standards are raised, and laws are passed. I can see a day when the use of synthetic chemicals is as unthinkable as smoking in an operating room.

After lunch, the kids hurry to their rooms to put on their swimsuits. It's 1 P.M., and the Ranch is nearly silent in the baking midsummer sun. A hot breeze rustles the leaves of the fledgling fruit trees that will, in a few years, help supply the kitchen. An Old West windmill turns lazily. A jackrabbit breaks across a pasture, his tail flashing white. At the slightest noise, the lizards on the rocks dart into their hiding places.

And then, here comes the noise: A pack of hot, exuberant kids bursts from the hacienda and heads for the pool. Rail-thin Ryan wins the sprint to the diving board and cannonballs into the water with a tremendous splash. We designed the pool to look like an old country swimming hole, with rocks from the nearby hills set right into the pool deck. Two massive boulders form a diving board. Within seconds, all the kids are in the water. Wyatt's right alongside them, at the moment pretending to be a horse, whinnying and rearing like a maverick.

Overhead, a row of puffy, fair-weather clouds meanders toward us. It's the daily cycle here on the front range of the Continental Divide. Moist air moves from the Pacific, forms clouds over the mountains, and tries to marshal a thunderstorm. Most days, nothing much comes of it. The rain tends to fall up in the high country, looking like plum-colored lace curtains from our distance. On this particular day, the sun shoots streaks through slanted drapes of faraway rain, like something right out of Cecil B. DeMille. The light dapples the valley and streaks the ridges. The sky out here is invariably beautiful.

When Don and I set up the Ranch, we knew we weren't experts on matters of child psychology or development. At Hackensack, there's an entire staff of well-trained professionals, expert in dealing with seriously ill or grieving children. All that is thanks to Erika Leeuwenburgh, the creator and founder of the child-life program at Hackensack University Medical Center, who understands children profoundly. Two of her child-life specialists arrive each week with the kids and spend the session on call around the clock, hard at work from dawn till dark and afterward. They're available for every kid facing every kind of need: comfort, advice, discipline, friendship. Child-life specialists keep the kids on schedule, remind them to slather on sunscreen, and listen with quiet understanding to any admissions of homesickness. They referee squabbles over the pool table and make sure that screen doors aren't left hanging open.

Part moms, part psychologists, part hall monitors, the child-life specialists are crucial to the operation of the Ranch.

After pool time, the kids get dressed and head back to work. Those who handled the horses in the morning are now assigned their afternoon chore duties, and vice versa. On many days, Andy and Edward take the kids for heavy-duty ranch work: clearing brush, chopping weeds, moving boulders. The kids love the hard work, and Andy and Edward are terrific role models who epitomize an authentic Western work ethic. This afternoon, however, they're spreading fresh sand outside the stalls with Chicken Jack. He scoops a load of sand in the front-end loader and dumps it where the kids can rake it flat. Then he moves to the next stall and the next, working down the length of the barn.

The other group begins their indoctrination in the rudiments of handling a horse: grooming, bridling, saddling. It's hard to believe that in just a day or two they'll be ready to head out with us on trail rides around the Ranch, but they will be.

One of my favorite rides takes us down through town and along an arroyo, across a pasture, and past the ruins of a long-abandoned ranch on this property. Finally, the ride takes us up a steep trail to the top of a rocky promontory we call Mountain Lion Mesa because we once saw one of the animals prowling the crest. A pair of red-tailed hawks have their aerie in the rocks near the top of the mesa, and sometimes as you near the spot, they'll suddenly appear in the sky, right at eye level, and then rise up effortlessly until they're floating in big circles a couple of hundred feet high. From there, they can survey most of the Ranch. I've seen them abruptly fold their wings and drop like bombs to hit prey near the old Santa Fe Trail.

On top of the mesa, you can find old arrowheads and shards left behind by tool-making Indians who lived on this land for centuries. You can imagine them up there still, looking down at the settlers' wagons creaking slowly toward them. I think of them waiting silently, watching, wondering, breathing in this same smell of piñon and cedar.

But before the kids can tackle Mountain Lion Mesa, they've got to learn to ride a simple circle around the rodeo arena. When the group is done bridling and saddling and walking their horses through town, there's just enough time to try some actual riding. Juan, a sturdy, round-faced little guy, is the first one up. He's already sitting atop Big John while, right next to him, Mariah is pleading with Molly: "Be gentle, horse. Please, be gentle." It turns out that Juan is a natural horseman. He sits relaxed but upright in the saddle, keeps his hands out over Big John's neck, and starts and stops the big brown horse as if he'd been a ranch hand all his life.

"When I saw him pick up the horse's feet to clean his shoes, I knew we could make a cowboy out of him," says Yunk about Juan. Most kids stand as far as they can get from the horses and stretch to reach the hooves: If the horse kicks, they want to be as far away as possible. But Juan settles his rear right next to Big John's knee, just like a pro. So it comes as no surprise when, after a few minutes of walking, Juan has Big John loping along happily.

But they don't have to be good at it to love riding. Julie looks almost petrified on Cinnamon's back. When she tries to stop, she says, "Whoa?" as if she's asking a favor. Something like relief passes over her face when it finally comes time to dismount—but no, that's just a sigh of joy. "I love it!" she says, smiling, and she presses her face into Cinnamon's flank.

By now you can see that the object of the Imus Ranch is not to have fun—although we do have a lot of fun. The purpose here is for the kids to grow and feel genuinely good about themselves by taking responsibility and latching on to a work ethic. Many of these kids have been coddled all their lives as though they're enfeebled, weak. They're defined by being *less* than other kids. We give them a chance to accomplish things for themselves, and they leave here knowing that they're just as good and just as able as anyone else.

We have a rule here: No one mentions that these children have cancer. And no one threatens them that way. They don't want you to feel sorry for them. And they don't want to be babied. They want you to know that they're normal.

A boy named Kenny came to visit us. He was 15 and had been diagnosed with brain tumors reaching down his spine. He had a drop foot and limited motion in his knees; a shunt had been installed in his skull near the right temple. His case was pretty severe.

For most of his life, Kenny had never been able to do any sports or even much of anything physical. He had to watch while other kids played. He got here, and we put him right to work as a ranch hand. The first time we went out riding, he only got halfway. He was in considerable pain and had to ride back in our ambulance, which is a camouflage-painted Humvee so the kids will think it's cool. Tim, our paramedic, follows us at a distance in the ambulance every time we hit the trail.

Kenny just wouldn't quit. The last day he was here, he made every step of a two-hour ride. It was amazing to see all willpower and determination. And when he got off that horse, he was crying. They were, however, tears of joy. It was a huge deal for him to have accomplished what he'd done.

That kid was truly extraordinary. He kept saying to us, "Thank you, thank you." Until I finally said, "No! *You* did that." He went home with a whole different perspective on his life, aware of the many things he could do instead of the things he couldn't do.

Kids need the dignity and the pride of doing for themselves. Don understands that because of the way he spent his formative years on that Arizona ranch. I learned it from my coaches and my parents. I've had a lot of coaches in my life, and the good ones were the ones who would not let me get away with anything short of my best. The good ones always know the difference.

※

As the week goes on and the kids improve their riding skills, we take them on more and more advanced rides. We now have trails snaking and climbing all over the Ranch and a huge choice of two- to three-hour rides. Some head up toward the mesa, an enormous block of sandstone and juniper that guards the Ranch like a fortress wall. We've built trails winding up the big hill with names like Sidewinder Mesa, Dueling Fences, Bear Cave Point, and Butch's Hideout. Or we can ride down slope from the town, along trails named Buffalo Ridge Lookout, Coyote Pass, Santa Fe Trail, and Barbed Wire Pass. On steep grades, the trails switch back and forth like a side-winding rattlesnake through surprisingly deep forests. Given enough water, the right soil, and nothing to stop them, juniper trees will cover an entire mountain in an almost impassable blanket. We have to clear some or the trees will suck the water table dry.

I'm partial to our mesa excursions, which we conduct by pickup truck. The switchbacks take us slowly up the mesa's steep sides, drives locked in "four wheel low." The air has a warm, piney fragrance, and the sound of our tires crunching along the exposed rock is almost hypnotic. Around one turn, there's a clearing that makes a nice place to stop. From this spot, we can look out over the valley where the brave Apache rode—until the wagon trains and iron locomotives pushed their way through the heart of Native American country. Beyond the valley lie ridges and ranges of mountains. It's a fabulous sight at any time of the day. Seen in the late afternoon, the valley and the mountains are a patchwork of light and dark greens and brown that shifts as the sun plays through the clouds.

The Ranch is nestled just below us. Slanting sunlight picks out a metal roof of one of the Ranch buildings and makes it glow, while the adobe of the hacienda looks as warm as freshly baked bread.

5 GREEN CLEANING AGENTS YOU PROBABLY HAVE AT HOME

Baking soda is a natural deodorizer that also acts as a scouring agent and a tub and tile cleaner in place of commercial scrubs. To keep your plumbing clog-free, pour equal parts baking soda and vinegar down the drain ($\frac{1}{2}$ cup of each is enough), let it sit for a half hour and then rinse with hot water. To polish silver, mix a pint of water with 3 pints of baking soda to form a paste. Apply it to your silver with a cloth, rinse under cold water, and wipe with a clean cloth to shine. (You can also use toothpaste the same way, as long as it's a paste, not a gel.)

Salt can be used to remove rust. Sprinkle the rusty spot with salt, squeeze lime juice over the salt, and allow it to sit for 3 hours. Use the lime rind to scrub off the rust.

Lemon juice can be used to clean copper sinks and pots and cut odors. To clean copper, mix a paste of lemon juice and baking soda, or lemon juice and salt. Use the juice from half a lemon in the wash cycle to get rid of odors.

White cider vinegar removes stains and cleans glass, coffeepots, and wooden floors. It can be used on countertop surfaces (except for marble). To disinfect your wooden floors and give them a beautiful shine, wash them once a week with 6 parts vinegar combined with 4 parts water and a squeeze of lemon juice. A tablespoon of white vinegar added to the rinse cycle also acts as a wonderful fabric softener.

Plants filter and remove airborne toxins from the environment without causing harm to themselves. Particularly in urban environments, house plants are extremely important, and spider plants—one of the easiest to grow—are among the most effective.

For more information about Greening the Cleaning products, log on to www.dienviro.com.

Once, Don and Yunk decided to ride their horses on ahead of us in the trucks to set up a trick for the kids. Before we set off, I told the kids that there are bears up on the mesa. It's true—we've seen them. Anyway, when we got to the mesa's top and stopped, we could hear trees rustling and movement in the brush. The kids looked at me nervously. We walked a bit, and the agitation off to the side grew louder. Then Don and Yunk, still out of sight, started making low growling noises. I halted the procession and ordered everyone to stay together. "Don't run," I said. Wyatt was in on the joke—and I think he may turn out to be quite the actor because he started pretending to be terrified. "Mommy, hold me!" he said.

Again, I warned everybody, "If it's a bear, *nobody run!*"

"Wait a minute . . . I *see* him!" one of the kids said.

"It's not a bear," another said. "It's *worse*. It's a wild boar!"

Finally, Don came out of the woods, laughing hard. The kids loved it. They couldn't believe that we'd jerked their chains that much. Just one example of the silly and fun stuff we do.

Sometimes driving up the mesa, I think about a girl named Leslie.

Leslie heard about our program and started writing letters to us, begging to visit the Imus Ranch. Her doctor said there was no way she could come. Leslie's condition made her prone to seizures and she had to take very heavy medication. I could see the doctor's point: If she had a seizure while on a horse, it could be life-threatening. She could fall, hit her head, frighten the animal, and even be trampled. But Leslie persisted and kept writing letters. "My dream," she wrote, "is to go to the Imus Ranch." I read one of Leslie's letters to David Jurist at the Tomorrows Children's Fund and told him that by not letting her come to the Ranch we were all potentially contributing to her depression. We talked it over and insisted that she be allowed to attend.

Well, finally, Leslie got permission. And we felt we could take care of her. Our doctor monitored her, and she was never far from the Humvee ambulance.

She loved the horses. We started Leslie in the indoor arena. Like all our kids, she wore a cowboy hat helmet. She looked like Elizabeth Taylor in *National Velvet*—seriously, she was just that stunning. Absolutely beautiful.

Leslie planted more vegetables than the other kids did. She pulled more weeds. From morning to evening, she worked harder than the rest because she had something to prove to herself and to us.

One day, she got up on a horse and rode with us in the arena. She was so proud—it was an enormous moment for her and everybody else. When I'm working my way up a steep, rocky trail somewhere, I think of the obstacles that girl has overcome, and I can't help but feel as if our vision for the Ranch, and what it can do, is coming true.

The top of the mesa is sort of surprising. *Mesa* means "tabletop" in Spanish, and that's exactly what it looks like: After you've made that long climb, suddenly everything you see is flat in all directions. We rest a bit, then hike around, and dream up games. The light clay dust is full of small miracles: arrowheads, shards of pottery—even an occasional meteorite! These are the tiny remains of iron blocks that soared through space and time until they hit the earth's atmosphere and shattered into thousands of fragments. Only the biggest chunks make it to the ground without burning up, and by the time they reach the surface, most are scarcely bigger than a marble.

But it's an amazing sight to see them coming. Out in the clear air of the Ranch, and far from the light pollution of cities, we see a lot of meteors trying to reach the ground. They're the shooting stars that streak across a clear western night, flashing past so quickly that you almost wonder whether you saw them at all. There's something magical about sending a kid home with a little piece of a shooting star.

Emma and Julie are curled up contentedly on the big window seat in the Great Room. It's 6 P.M., and outside the windows, the kiln of the midday summer has softened into a warm evening brace. Twelve hours of hard work has the kids feeling tired—and happily satisfied. Wyatt and Harlan are playing chess on the big table between two sofas. Other kids are scattered through the hacienda, enjoying a few spare moments in a demanding, exhilarating day. A few are in the library, playing chess there or lounging on the kilim chaise.

Suppertime brings everybody to the table. Don tweaks the stereo a bit and the room fills with the music of the Flatlanders. The kids pick up their plates and look over the offerings laid out on the sideboards in spacious platters and big bowls. Eating healthy should never feel like a sacrifice or a compromise, and this dinner once again shows just how much is possible. The menu starts with thick submarine sandwiches, stuffed with fresh organic greens and organic soy "turkey" and "cheese." There's a hearty spinach soup, crunchy homemade croutons, and a plate of tender bok choy from the greenhouse. The homemade crinkle-sliced potato chips prove that anything you can buy in an unhealthy foil bag can be done in a healthier, better-tasting way at home.

After supper, the kids pile into one of the pickup trucks to visit the town's Bull and Bear Dance Hall for an hour or so of shooting pool, playing poker and pinball, and listening to the jukebox. These kids have put in a long day, and they know they'll be up again with the dawn.

It's after 8 P.M. now, and the sun's dropped below the far ridge. Dark storm clouds, having spent all day gathering, now hang in the western half of the sky. Lighter clouds overhead pick up the last rays of sunshine and reflect them back in cotton-candy colors. It's all a wonder to watch.

Looking back, I'd have to say that Don and I didn't know for sure what we were getting into when we built the Imus Ranch. The entire project was something so new. Yes, we sketched it all on napkins and Don described our ideas to his listeners—but we couldn't be sure at all that people would really respond. It truly was a leap of faith. And it just came together. Designing and building the Ranch, we felt sort of like jazz musicians, I guess—we knew where we wanted to end up, but we weren't quite sure how we would get there. It has been an improvisation but has never diverged from the theme of healthy living in harmony with self-reliance.

Before any kid is chosen to come to the Ranch, he or she has to fill out a survey, and one of the questions we ask is: What are your responsibilities at home? You'd be surprised how many kids answer: "None." Their parents mean well. They have had to live with the chance that they could lose their child, so of course they bend over backward to indulge, pamper, and protect them. But Don and I realize that kids want to know that they're helping and capable. They want to know that they have value. So if someone wonders, "How did you come up with all of this?" the answer is that we didn't really think about it or ponder it or brood over it. Without really having to have a lot of heavy discussion, Don and I were on the same page.

The same napkin.

For me, it's beyond rewarding. I treasure the chance to watch these kids grow and change, to learn from them, and to draw strength from them and the chance to share what I've learned over a lifetime of reading and experimenting with healthy, nontoxic alternatives to the poisonous environmental conditions most people unwittingly tolerate.

I hope this book will give you ideas and encouragement to green your own lifestyle the way we have done at the Imus Ranch. Remember: You don't have to do everything at once. Just take the first step—or if you're already on the path, take the next step. You can do more than you might think.

the imus ranch vegan pantry

ALL THE FRUITS, VEGETABLES, AND GRAINS WE USE AT THE RANCH ARE COMPLETELY ORGANIC. THAT MEANS EVERYTHING HAS BEEN GROWN WITHOUT USING CHEMICALS (SUCH AS PESTICIDES, FUNGICIDES, OR FERTILIZERS), ACCORDING TO ENVIRONMENTALLY SOUND PRACTICES.

It's because we believe organic food is best able to sustain our health and the health of our planet. In addition, we try to make sure all the products we use are organic, free of any additives, and in their purest form.

To help you and your family navigate the choices, we've put together the following list of the foods we use most frequently, many of which are used in the recipes that appear in this book. We've included explanations of those that might be unfamiliar to you and, where appropriate, the brands we prefer. The list is not intended to be all inclusive, nor do we mean to imply that there aren't other brands you might prefer or find easier to obtain. Those we mention are ones we have researched, tasted, and cooked with, so we recommend them with confidence. These are, however, only guidelines that we hope will be helpful, especially if the vegan lifestyle is new for you.

Beverages

Water All the water at the Ranch is filtered by means of reverse osmosis, a system installed beneath the sink that removes virtually all contaminants. If you're not ready to install such a system, there are various kinds of inexpensive options you can use: Buy filtered water; install a filter on your tap; or buy a Brita filtering carafe and be sure to change the filter as recommended. Distilled water is not the best option for children because the distilling process removes essential minerals along with contaminants.

Juices For drinking and cooking, we use a variety of organic juice concentrates from Cascadian Farm. Because concentrates require smaller packaging, they're easier to store than regular juice. We also find a lot of uses for R. W. Knudsen's Very Veggie Vegetable Cocktail.

Fruit-flavored drinks One slight exception to our all-organic rule is that we serve Gatorade at every meal. It's noncarbonated and provides many essential minerals that can be depleted as the visiting ranch hands complete their chores.

Teas and coffee We serve only organic herbal teas, and with so many wonderful flavors available, we always seem to have a great selection on hand. As for coffee, we serve our own dark blend of Imus Ranch coffee (see page 59 for ordering information). Coffee is one of the intensively farmed agricultural crops, so be sure that the coffee you buy is made from organic beans, too.

Binders and Thickeners

Agar-agar This tasteless form of dried seaweed is widely used in Asia as a texturizing agent, emulsifier, stabilizing agent, and thickener. It's popularly used as a vegetarian alternative to gelatin. We find it's a wonderful addition to our Imus Ranch Hollandaise Sauce (page 129).

Arrowroot Sold as a tasteless powder, arrowroot is used as a thickener for cooking sauces and puddings; it has approximately twice the thickening power of flour. Because arrowroot becomes clear when cooked, it's the perfect thickener in Buckley's Lemon Meringue Tart (page 228).

Breads, Grains, Cereals, and Pasta

Bread We favor whole-grain breads because they pack the most fiber and nutrients into every slice. All the bread we use at the Ranch is made by Rudi's Rustics and is completely organic. We even use these breads to make our own croutons and bread crumbs.

Cellophane noodles Also known as glass or bean-thread noodles, cellophane noodles are actually made from the starch of mung beans and are widely used in Chinese, Thai, and other Asian cuisines. Because they are actually cooked before they are dried, these noodles need only to soak in warm water before they're ready to use in a recipe. We use Eden Foods brand in our dishes.

Cereal A high-fiber breakfast is a sure way to give young ranch hands a good start to their day. We serve Kashi Go Lean Crunch and Raspberry Rhapsody cereals made by Health Valley.

Flour Even though we buy most of our bread, we still find all kinds of uses many different kinds of flour in our cooking. In addition to unbleached white flour and pastry flour, we also use whole wheat, buckwheat, rye, and spelt flour. The brand we prefer is Arrowhead.

Pasta Most kids (both young and old) seem to love pasta, so we try to keep a wide variety on hand at all times—that often includes shells, ziti, linguini, lasagna, and fettuccine, all made with organic semolina.

Quinoa It's an ancient grain that has been called the perfect protein because it contains all eight essential amino acids. We use it in many of the dishes served at the Ranch.

Rice In addition to unbleached long-grain white rice and long- and short-grain brown rice, we also use arborio, a short-grain white rice with a high starch content, and wehani, a particularly aromatic variety of brown rice, as well as unbleached white and brown basmati rice and jasmine rice. Lundberg is our favorite brand.

Tortillas In Mexico, tortillas are a staple served daily—here at the Ranch, they're served not quite as often, but sometimes the table just doesn't seem complete without them. We prefer Rudi's Rustic Organic Tortillas, as well as our own Imus Ranch Turquoise Buffalo Tortilla Chips (see page 59).

Dairy Substitutes

AS ALTERNATIVES TO BUTTER

Olive oil Equally delicious as a cooking ingredient as it is on a slice of bread, olive oil is a perfect alternative to butter. It's loaded with monounsaturated fats and full of flavor. We use Spectrum Naturals brand.

Trans fats free margarine The new "trans fats free" label that's appearing on more and more margarine tubs means that the product doesn't contain trans-fatty acids, a dangerous form of fat that has been linked to heart disease. Look for "expeller-pressed" on the label, which means that the oils were extracted without using solvents. The brand we prefer is called Spectrum Spread. Look for it in health food stores or your local supermarket.

AS ALTERNATIVES TO CHEESE

Rice cheese Made from rice milk, rice cheese is a soy-free alternative that's low-fat, cholesterol-free, and lactose-free and is fortified with essential vitamins and minerals. We usually have rice Parmesan from Tree of Life on hand.

Soy cheese With a wealth of soy cheese so widely available, we keep all the common favorites in our refrigerator—cheddar, Swiss, and mozzarella. Soya Kaas is the brand we use. We also like SoyCo grated Parmesan cheese in our Penne Primavera with Cream Sauce (page 180).

Rice milk We use rice milk, which is made from organic brown rice, in a wide range of dishes. We prefer Rice Dream's enriched products because they're fortified to contain as much calcium and vitamins A and D as cow's milk does. It's available in original, vanilla, and carob flavors.

Soy milk Soy milk is one organic product that's really going mainstream. Perhaps because so many people are lactose-intolerant, a wide variety of brands seem to crowd dairy shelves everywhere. Extra Eden is our favorite brand—fortified with extra vitamins and minerals, it comes in original, vanilla, and carob flavors.

Rice and soy-based frozen desserts Because these products are dairy-free, they're technically not ice cream. But, names aside, you'd be hard pressed to find fault with these luscious, creamy desserts, and you don't need to travel far to find them. They're widely available in the frozen foods sections of health food stores. Rice Dream and Soy Dream brands are what we prefer—the only hard part is finding a favorite flavor.

Eggs and Egg Substitutes

Organic eggs We use only the eggs from our chickens, which are fed organically. Organic eggs are widely available now in many supermarkets. It is important to use large eggs in all our recipes because the volume of the yolk and white makes a difference in the outcome of the dish.

Bananas In many baking recipes, we've found that ½ cup mashed banana can replace one egg with perfect results. It's also a great way to use up bananas that have become soft and dark.

Egg-substitute products Wonderslim is a liquid egg substitute that works particularly well in our salad dressings. Two tablespoons is the equivalent of one egg. In baking and cooking, we prefer to use Ener-G Egg Replacer. It's a wheat-free, dairy-free powder that is mixed with water. Both are available in health food stores.

Flaxseeds We keep flaxseeds on hand for making another easy egg substitution. Just mix 1 tablespoon ground flaxseeds with ¼ cup water to form a paste that can be used in baking to replace one egg. Flaxseeds, in addition to providing high-quality, easily digested protein, are also a good source of omega-3 linolenic acid. Flaxseeds can turn rancid easily, so it's best to store them in the refrigerator and grind as needed.

Tofu In many recipes, we use tofu in place of eggs to lend a thick and creamy consistency to a dish. For more on tofu, see "Soybeans" on page 58.

Vegan mayonnaise Instead of real mayonnaise in our salads and sandwiches, we often use a spread called Veganaise, a dairy- and egg-free substitute that comes in four varieties. The one we use is expeller-pressed, which means that the oil used in the product is extracted without the use of solvents. And because it doesn't contain eggs or dairy, you don't have to refrigerate it.

Flavorings, Seasonings, and Soup Bases

Chipotle chiles in adobo sauce Chipotle chiles are jalapeños that have been smoked and dried; adobo sauce is a thick paste made of ground chiles, herbs, and vinegar. Together they come in jars or cans. We use the preparation frequently because they lend such a distinct smoky flavor to foods, and it's easy to control how much heat they lend a dish. Once opened, store leftover chipotles in the refrigerator.

Herbs and spices At the Ranch we make every effort to use fresh herbs in our cooking whenever possible. But when fresh ones aren't available, we turn to dried (we seem to use thyme, dill, and oregano most frequently). In our recipes, we use these basics: allspice, basil, black pepper, Cajun seasoning, cayenne, cinnamon, clove, coriander, cumin, dill, garlic powder, ginger, granulated garlic, nutmeg, onion powder, oregano, paprika, rosemary, sage, thyme, and turmeric. As you build your own collection of favorite dried seasonings, remember to store them in a cool, dark place to maintain maximum freshness. We prefer Frontier brand.

Essential oils In recipes that call for grated citrus zest, the zest is usually a critical ingredient because it contains the citrus oils that add pure flavor to a dish. For convenience, many of our recipes rely on a few drops of lemon oil instead of grated zest. If you use essential oils, be careful to buy products specifically labeled for use in cooking (aromatherapy oils are not food-grade). The brand we use is Dr. Young's.

Extracts These are concentrated seasonings that are used to impart intense flavor without adding volume to a dish. Almond and vanilla are the two we use most often, mainly in baking. We prefer to use Frontier brand because they're alcohol-free.

Salt At the Ranch, we use sea salt and kosher salt. As the name implies, sea salt is the by-product of evaporating seawater, so it contains more trace minerals than regular table salt.

Soy sauce and tamari These are the sauces used in Asian cooking that we use to flavor many dishes at the Ranch. Both impart a nice saltiness, but with an added nutty dimension.

Vegetable broth We find plenty of opportunities to use soup bases in our recipes (even when we're not making soup) because they add such a nice flavor to foods. We cook with Morga Vegetable Bouillon a lot; we also like to use Seitenbacher Instant Vegetable Broth Mix, which comes in powdered form and is easier to add to a dish in small amounts.

Legumes

Beans We consider beans one of the most important staples in our pantry. They turn up in a lot of dishes inspired by our local Southwestern cuisine, from soups to burritos. But we love them so much we've found all kinds of new uses for them, too. We keep a varied supply of dried organic beans on hand, which usually includes the following: black beans, black-eyed peas, chickpeas (also known as garbanzo beans), kidney beans, pinto beans, and split peas. We also use canned beans from Westbrae Natural, Health Valley, and Eden Foods. Of course, soybeans are another essential pantry item. For more on edamame and tofu, see the entry on soy on page 58; for information on great soy-based products, see "Dairy Substitutes" on page 53 and "Meat Substitutes" below.

Lentils Used throughout many cuisines worldwide, lentils have a fair amount of calcium and are a good source of iron and phosphorus. Never purchased fresh, they're always dried, so they'll keep well for a year or so if stored in an airtight container. We like to have a good supply of both red and green lentils on hand.

Meat Substitutes

AS ALTERNATIVES TO BEEF

Seitan Known in this country by its Japanese name (pronounced *say-tan*), seitan is an extremely versatile product made of cooked wheat gluten and soy that is high in protein, low in fat, and has an amazing ability to mimic the taste and texture of beef. We like to slather it with barbeque sauce and stuff it into tacos, but depending on how you season it, seitan can also resemble chicken pretty easily.

Textured soy protein (TSP) and textured vegetable protein (TVP) Used as alternatives to ground beef, these products are good sources of fiber and a high-quality protein. They're made with defatted soy flour that has been processed and dried to give a substance with a spongelike texture that may be flavored to resemble meat, but it is commonly sold unflavored. We use Bob's Red Mill brand for both TSP and TVP.

Vegetable burgers There are so many great ways to dress up a vegetable burger. When the urge for one strikes, we often reach for our own Imus Ranch Barbecue Sauce (page 127) or a nice ripe avocado. SuperBurgers, by Turtle Island Foods, is one of our favorite brands.

AS ALTERNATIVES TO PORK

Soy bacon Leading a vegan lifestyle doesn't mean you have to stop enjoying the flavor of bacon. We use a soy-based product called Fakin' Bacon, made by Lightlife, that cooks and tastes just like bacon. We also use it to make Salad Bits 'n Bits (page 146).

Soy sausage In addition to being a significantly lower in fat than pork sausages, vegetarian sausages are a great source of protein. We use Gimme Lean, by Lightlife, for its great flavor.

AS ALTERNATIVES TO POULTRY

Soy chicken We use a vegetable protein "chicken" breast that can be used in all the ways you'd use a skinless and boneless breast. It's especially good in our Waldorf salad. The brand we prefer is Veat.

Soy turkey Made from a protein and wheat blend that has the texture and flavor of turkey, we never have to wait for Thanksgiving to enjoy a few slices of soy turkey on a sandwich. The brand we use is Tofurky, which is made by Turtle Island Foods.

Nuts and Seeds

Nuts Nutritional powerhouses, most nuts are high in calcium, folic acid, magnesium, vitamin E, and fiber, so we like to keep a wide variety in the Ranch pantry for snacks and cooking. Our favorites include: almonds, hazelnuts, macadamia nuts, pecans, pine nuts, and walnuts. (We do not use peanuts, which are actually legumes, because so many people are highly allergic to them.) To ensure the best flavor, we store them airtight and toast them lightly in a dry skillet until fragrant before using.

Seeds Offering many of the same nutrition benefits as nuts, seeds provide another great way add a pleasant nutty crunch to dishes. We keep a wide variety in our pantry, including flaxseeds, pumpkin seeds, sesame seeds, and sunflower seeds.

Oils and Vinegars

Oil When it comes to oil, a one-size-fits-all philosophy flies out the window. In fact, we typically have at least six different oils in the pantry because each plays such a distinct role in our menu. For example, we mostly use cold-pressed extra-virgin olive oil for cooking (and sometimes in making salad dressings when we want its flavor to come through). But we use walnut oil and hazelnut oil in our baking because they have a blander flavor that won't overpower the other ingredients. Sesame oil is used to give Asian-inspired dishes their distinct, nutty flavor; and both sunflower and safflower oil frequently show up in our salad dressings and sauces. All the oils we use at the Ranch are made by Spectrum Naturals.

Vinegar The familiar tang that perks up many dishes is often the result of a splash of vinegar added at just the right time. In particular, the most common uses we find for vinegar are in our salad dressings. We like using brown-rice vinegar when we want a mild and smooth sour taste, and balsamic vinegar when a stronger, sweeter taste is desired. As with our oils, we use Spectrum Naturals brand.

Relishes and Condiments

Capers These little delicacies are actually brine-cured flower buds that are a distinct part of Mediterranean cooking. They range in size and come in varieties as large as the tip of your little finger to the nonpareil (extra-small) variety that we prefer. The brand we like is Cascadian Farm.

Ketchup What could make a veggie burger better than adding a nice thick squirt of ketchup? We use Muir Glen brand.

Mustard An essential part of any picnic plan, we use mustard in everything from potato salad to sloppy joes. For those reasons and more, we typically keep a good quantity of yellow, spicy brown, and Dijon mustard in the pantry. The brand we use is Natural Value.

Olives The color of an olive is in part determined by when it is picked off the branch. Underripe olives are always green, but the color deepens as the fruit matures and will sometimes become quite dark and even black if allowed to become truly ripe. Not surprisingly, these factors affect the flavor as will the way the olive was cured and packed. It's hard to find a favorite with so many wonderful olives to choose from, but we prefer the pitted ripe olives from Natural Value and stuffed green olives from Cascadian Farm.

Pickles Technically, any food that has been preserved in a vinegar or brine solution can qualify as a type of pickle, but here we're talking about the classic pickled cucumber. We like ours a number ways: sliced and sweet, as kosher dills, and chopped into sweet relish. The brand we use is Cascadian Farm.

Worchestershire sauce This condiment imparts such a distinct flavor, a number of our favorite dishes wouldn't be the same without it. We use it in our Cowboy Sloppy Joes (page 160) and Imus Ranch Barbecue Sauce (page 127). The traditional recipe for this sauce calls for anchovies, but we always make sure to use a vegan brand, such as the Vegetarian Worchestershire Sauce by the Wizard.

Soybeans

Edamame All soy products are not created equal. We use tofu, tempeh, seitan, miso, and soy sauce on the Ranch. These products do not contain soy isolates or hydrolyzed soy protein, which you should avoid. With their popularity increasing, soybeans are commonly known in this country by their Japanese name, *edamame*. It is in fact a word for a particular variety of soybean that's harvested while still in the green stage. Edamame look very much like peas in their pod. Steamed or blanched, sprinkled with a bit of sea salt while still hot, they are delicious popped from their shells and eaten out of hand.

Tofu You may be more familiar with soybeans as bean curd. Tofu is made from curdled soymilk extracted from ground cooked soybeans and processed in a way that is similar to cheese-making. The firmness is determined by how much of the whey has been pressed out of the curds in the process. We use soft, firm, and extra-firm Mori-Nu brand silken tofu, which has an extremely delicate and smooth texture.

Sweets and Sweeteners

Brown-rice syrup An extremely versatile and healthy sweetener, brown-rice syrup provides a more steady stream of energy because it takes longer for the body to process than many other natural sweeteners. With a shelf life of about a year, this syrup should be stored in a cool, dry place once opened. We use Lundberg and Sweet Cloud brands in our dishes.

Carob Because its taste is so similar to that of chocolate, carob is a great substitute in many of our recipes. But unlike chocolate, it contains no caffeine, so carob powder is a kid-friendly product to have on hand for late-night cups of cocoa. The chips we use are made by Sunspire.

Chocolate Aside from the traditional cookie uses, we melt Sunspire brand chocolate chips at the Ranch to make chocolate frostings and hot chocolate. Among our favorite products is dark chocolate Bug Bites. Made from all natural and organic ingredients by the Endangered Species Chocolate Company, each package also includes trading cards with messages about the benefits of organic gardening.

Maple syrup We use only grade B maple syrup, the darkest, most intensely flavored grade, which is processed in open kettles without formaldehyde. It's the best sweetener and the most balanced sugar, containing positive and negative ions.

Raw unrefined sugar Instead of white or brown sugar, we prefer to use a brand of organic sugar called Sucanat. It's sugar in its most natural form, free of any additives or preservatives. To make it, juice is extracted from organically grown sugarcane and evaporated according to a special Swiss formula so only the water is removed; a sugar with a light molasses flavor remains. We also use turbinado sugar, which has a different consistency and color. Sucanat is good for certain baked goods because it doesn't brown too much under heat, while turbinado sugar is good for caramelized foods and cookies.

Tomato Products

Canned tomatoes We love to use canned tomatoes in our cooking because they save a lot of time. And because we use an organic brand that tastes so incredibly fresh, Muir Glen, it's hard to tell the difference between canned and fresh when you taste the final dish. We use both its fire-roasted diced tomatoes and crushed tomatoes with basil in a number of our recipes.

Ketchup See Relishes and Condiments on page 57.

Juice See Beverages on page 52.

Pastes and sauces Our baked ziti wouldn't taste the same without the Tomato-Basil Sauce by Muir Glen. Its garden-fresh taste sets it apart from a lot of other products on the shelf. And if we should ever run out, we always have a can of tomato paste of the same brand tucked away; we simply thin it down to get the right consistency.

Imus Ranch Products

For more information on purchasing Imus Ranch foods, such as Imus Ranch Southwest Salsa and Imus Ranch Turquoise Buffalo Tortilla Chips, visit the Web site at www.imusranchfoods.com.

Orange Poppy Seed Muffins (page 64)

breads and breakfast foods

WHETHER YOUR DAY IS GOING TO BE SPENT WORKING ON A RANCH, IN AN OFFICE, AT SCHOOL, OR IN THE HOME, BREAKFAST IS THE MEAL THAT PROVIDES THE FUEL TO KEEP YOU GOING.

A sugary doughnut, muffin, or commercial cereal in the morning offers a sudden rise in blood sugar and the quick burst of energy that it comes with it, but it usually provides little real nutrition and you'll just as surely crash long before it's time for lunch. A bowl of our Rio Grande Granola (page 68), a stack of Butch's Blueberry Pancakes (page 75), or our Strawberry Whole-Grain Waffles (page 77), on the other hand, will not only wake you up but also give you energy for hours.

Even the breads, muffins, and biscuits in this chapter offer the health benefits of organic unbleached flour without refined sugar and empty calories, so you can enjoy them whenever you want.

Cheesy Cheddar Biscuits

Serve these for breakfast with scrambled eggs and soy sausage or as an accompaniment to almost any soup. They're also great as an alternative crust for the Broccoli and Edamame Casserole (page 184).

2⅓	CUPS UNBLEACHED WHITE FLOUR	1	CUP PLUS 2 TABLESPOONS SOY MILK OR ORGANIC
4	TEASPOONS BAKING POWDER		MILK
½	TEASPOON BAKING SODA	¾	CUP GRATED SOY CHEDDAR CHEESE OR CHEDDAR
1	TEASPOON SALT		CHEESE
4	TABLESPOONS TRANS FATS FREE MARGARINE		

Preheat the oven to 375°F. Stir 2 cups of the flour, the baking powder, baking soda, and salt together in a mixing bowl. Cut in the margarine until the mixture forms coarse crumbs. Add the milk and cheese and stir just until the mixture forms a dough. Do not overmix.

Sprinkle your work surface with the remaining flour, roll out the dough to a thickness of ½ inch, and cut out 10 biscuits with a biscuit cutter. Arrange the biscuits so they are slightly touching one another on an ungreased baking sheet, and bake for 15 minutes, or until they are nicely browned on top. Serve warm or at room temperature.

MAKES 10 BISCUITS

Orange Poppy Seed Muffins

These are really popular when we serve them for breakfast at the Ranch. Try them at home—they're quick to make, and the kids and cowboys at your house will like them as much as ours do.

	SUNFLOWER OR SAFFLOWER OIL,	⅔	CUP RICE MILK OR ORGANIC MILK
	FOR BRUSHING MUFFIN CUPS	2	TABLESPOONS UNDILUTED ORANGE JUICE
1¼	CUPS UNBLEACHED WHITE FLOUR		CONCENTRATE
2	TEASPOONS BAKING POWDER	½	TEASPOON VANILLA EXTRACT
1	TABLESPOON OLIVE OIL	2	TABLESPOONS POPPY SEEDS
¼	CUP HONEY		
1	EGG		

Preheat the oven to 350°F. Brush the insides of 10 muffin cups with sunflower or safflower oil.

Combine the flour and baking powder in a medium bowl, stir to mix well, and set aside. In a separate bowl, combine all the remaining ingredients except the poppy seeds. Pour the wet ingredients into the bowl with the flour–baking powder mixture and stir until well blended. Sprinkle the poppy seeds over the batter and stir to distribute them evenly. Spoon the batter into the prepared muffin cups and bake 20 to 30 minutes, until the muffins are golden brown.

MAKES 10 MUFFINS

My Time at the Imus Ranch

ASHLEY BOONE

Beep! Beep! Beep! 5:30 A.M. I wake up abruptly, pulling my hand out of the warm covers to shut the alarm off. I wonder why the heck I am voluntarily getting up at this hour during the summer. My eyes open again and I call over to my roommate, Leslie, to see whether she's awake. Within a few minutes, we are ready to go. When we venture to the other side of the hacienda, we find Don, wide awake, drinking coffee, and watching the news. When everyone else is ready, he drives us down to the barn in his truck.

First we feed the animals, and then we team up for chores. Twenty minutes later, everyone is munching breakfast as the sun begins to make its trip across the sky. Afterward, half the group goes with Donnie to work with the horses, and the other half goes to work on another part of the Ranch.

On this day, I'm going to ride a horse by myself for the first time. After everyone else is saddled up, Woody the horse waits patiently as Donnie and I get the sleek, stiff leather saddle ready. As I put tension on the rein and guide Woody around, we make an instant connection. When I get in the saddle, I am 15 hands above the ground! Throughout the week the bond between Woody and me slowly grew; I learned to give him clear signals about what I want, like turning right or stepping.

Now I remember why I didn't mind getting up so early—the sooner you get up, the more time you have to enjoy the day.

Lemon Flaxseed Quick Bread

You can pile slices of this delicious quick bread in a breadbasket for breakfast or lunch, or serve it as a dessert with ice cream, fresh fruit, or both. The possibilities are endless.

¼	CUP SAFFLOWER OR SUNFLOWER OIL, PLUS MORE FOR OILING PANS	2	TEASPOONS GOLDEN FLAXSEEDS, GROUND FINELY
2¼	CUPS UNBLEACHED WHITE FLOUR	1	TEASPOON BAKING SODA
¾	CUP WHOLE-WHEAT FLOUR	½	TEASPOON SALT
1½	CUPS RAW UNREFINED SUGAR	1	CUP RICE MILK OR ORGANIC MILK
2	TABLESPOONS GRATED LEMON ZEST	¼	CUP FRESH LEMON JUICE
		2	TEASPOONS RICE VINEGAR

Preheat the oven to 350°F. Lightly oil an 8-by-4-inch loaf pan. Combine the flours, sugar, lemon zest, flaxseeds, baking soda, and salt in a large bowl. Mix well. Whisk together the rice milk, lemon juice, ¼ cup oil, and vinegar. Stir liquid ingredients into the flour mixture until just blended.

Pour the batter into the prepared pan and bake 50 to 55 minutes, until the quick bread is golden on top and a toothpick inserted in center comes out clean. Cool on wire rack before cutting into 12 slices.

MAKES 12 SERVINGS

Imus Ranch Garlic Bread

Serve this delicious, crunchy bread with pasta, or anything else you like. As far as I'm concerned, garlic bread goes with everything!

1	LOAF CRUSTY BREAD (YOUR CHOICE)
¼	CUP TRANS FATS FREE MARGARINE, SOFTENED
2	TO 3 MEDIUM CLOVES GARLIC, MINCED
¼ TO ½	TEASPOON SALT
	PAPRIKA, TO TASTE

Preheat the oven to 350°F. Slice the bread ¼ to ½ inch thick and arrange it on a baking sheet large enough to hold all the slices in a single layer. Mix the minced garlic with the softened margarine. Spread the slices evenly with the margarine mixture, and dust them with the salt and paprika. Bake about 25 minutes, until the bread is toasted and the margarine has melted.

MAKES 1 LARGE LOAF

Rio Grande Granola

Everybody at the Ranch loves this granola. It has a slightly chewy texture, a fragrant spicy taste, and just the right amount of sweetness. Before baking, the mixture is somewhat sticky, so use a big wooden spoon to stir it. Store in an airtight container until ready to use.

2	CUPS ROLLED OATS		1	TABLESPOON GROUND CINNAMON
1/4	CUP RAW UNREFINED SUGAR		1/8	TEASPOON GROUND GINGER
1/4	CUP RAISINS		1/4	CUP SAFFLOWER OIL
1/4	CUP TOASTED ALMONDS		1	TO 2 TABLESPOONS HONEY
1/4	CUP SLICED DEHYDRATED BANANA (OPTIONAL)		1/2	TEASPOON VANILLA EXTRACT

Preheat the oven to 300°F. Combine the oats, sugar, raisins, almonds, banana, cinnamon, and ginger in a large mixing bowl; stir until blended. In a separate bowl, stir together the oil, honey, and vanilla. Add the wet mixture to the dry mixture and stir with a wooden spoon until well blended.

Spread the mixture in a thin even layer on a large baking sheet and bake 30 to 35 minutes, until lightly browned, stirring it twice and then patting down with a spatula. Scrape the granola onto a clean baking sheet and set aside to cool.

MAKES SIX 1/2-CUP SERVINGS

Fresh Fruit Blintzes

The tender, delicate pancakes will keep for three or four days in the refrigerator. Lay them flat and separate each with a sheet of waxed paper. Then wrap them airtight. Serve the blintzes with fruit filling or warm maple syrup.

FOR THE BLINTZES

- ½ CUP UNBLEACHED WHITE FLOUR
- ⅛ TEASPOON BAKING SODA
- ⅓ TEASPOON BAKING POWDER
- ¾ CUP RICE MILK OR ORGANIC MILK
- 1 TABLESPOON HONEY
- 1 TABLESPOON TRANS FATS FREE MARGARINE, MELTED
- 1 EGG
- 2 TABLESPOONS WATER
- SAFFLOWER OIL, FOR OILING PAN
- ¼ CUP TRANS FATS FREE MARGARINE, MELTED

FOR THE FILLING

- 1 CUP FRESH RASPBERRIES
- 1 CUP FRESH BLUEBERRIES
- 1 CUP FRESH STRAWBERRIES
- 1 CUP FRESH BLACKBERRIES
- 1 CUP RAW UNREFINED SUGAR
- 2 TEASPOONS GRATED LEMON ZEST
- ½ TEASPOON VANILLA EXTRACT

To make the blintz batter, stir together the flour, baking soda, and baking powder. In a separate bowl, combine the rice milk, honey, margarine, and egg. Add the wet ingredients to the flour mixture and stir to combine. The batter should be the consistency of heavy cream. Set aside.

To prepare the filling, combine the berries, sugar, zest, vanilla, and water in a mixing bowl and toss to blend well.

Preheat the oven to 200°F. Oil a stainless steel pan with a bit of safflower oil and set it over medium heat. Ladle ¼ cup of the batter into the pan, tilting the pan to spread the batter evenly. Cook for 1 minute, until the batter is set and the bottom is browned. Turn the blintz and cook 15 to 20 seconds on the other side. Transfer to a flat plate and spread it with approximately 2 tablespoons of the filling. Turn in the 2 opposite ends and roll up the blintz. Transfer it, seam side down, to a baking sheet, brush the top with a bit of the melted margarine, and then put in the oven to keep warm. Repeat the procedure until all the batter and filling is used.

MAKES 4 TO 6 SERVINGS

Tofu Banana French Toast

Here's a terrific twist on a popular kid favorite: Serve this sweet and hearty breakfast as we do at the Ranch with maple syrup, Raspberry-Banana Puree (page 240), or any fruit preserve.

1	POUND SILKEN TOFU		1	TEASPOON GROUND CINNAMON
¼	CUP RICE MILK OR ORGANIC MILK		¼	CUP WATER
½	CUP RAW UNREFINED SUGAR		1	CUP MASHED BANANA
1	TEASPOON VANILLA EXTRACT		8	THICK SLICES BREAD
¼	CUP HONEY		¼	CUP SUNFLOWER OR SAFFLOWER OIL

Combine all the ingredients except the bread and the oil in the container of a blender and blend until smooth; it should have a batterlike consistency. Transfer the mixture to a bowl and dip the bread slices into the batter to coat all sides. Brush a frying pan with the oil and set it over medium heat. When the pan is hot, fry the bread until golden brown on both sides, approximately 3 to 4 minutes per side.

SERVES 4

Buckwheat Apple Flapjacks

Buckwheat is loaded with nutrients, especially protein, and this flour has been used in Asia for noodle-making for hundreds of years. Top these tasty flapjacks with berries, drizzle them with maple syrup, and serve them with tempeh bacon strips for a delicious breakfast.

1	CUP BUCKWHEAT FLOUR	2	CUPS WATER
1	CUP UNBLEACHED WHITE FLOUR	2	SMALL RED APPLES (SUCH AS DELICIOUS), PEELED, CORED, AND DICED
1	TEASPOON BAKING POWDER		WALNUT OIL, FOR OILING PAN
2	EGGS		
1	TEASPOON VANILLA EXTRACT		

Combine the flours and baking powder in a bowl and stir to mix well. Add the eggs, vanilla, and water; mix to blend, making sure to get all the lumps out without overmixing. Stir in the apples.

Heat a griddle or a large stainless steel pan over medium heat. When the oil is shimmering, ladle ¼ cup of batter onto the pan and cook 2 to 3 minutes, until the top of the flapjack is bubbly. Flip the flapjack with a spatula and cook on the other side 2 to 3 minutes, until golden. Continue to oil the pan and cook the flapjacks until all the batter is used.

MAKES 12 FLAPJACKS

Butch's Blueberry Pancakes

Plump, dark purple blueberries are rich in vitamin C, iron, potassium, and magnesium, and they're absolutely delicious the way they burst with flavor in these light and airy pancakes. We like to serve these with either maple syrup or a fruit syrup.

3	CUPS UNBLEACHED WHITE FLOUR	1	EGG
1	TABLESPOON BAKING POWDER	1	TABLESPOON MAPLE SYRUP
½	TEASPOON SALT	2⅓	TO 3 CUPS VANILLA RICE MILK OR ORGANIC MILK
1	TABLESPOON CINNAMON	1	CUP FRESH BLUEBERRIES, RINSED AND STEMMED
2	TABLESPOONS HONEY	¼	CUP SUNFLOWER OR SAFFLOWER OIL

Sift the flour, baking powder, salt, and cinnamon together into a medium mixing bowl. In a small mixing bowl, whisk together the honey, egg, maple syrup, and rice milk. Add the wet ingredients to the dry ingredients and whisk to dissolve any lumps. There may be a few beads of flour left in the batter, but they will dissolve in cooking. Fold the blueberries into the batter and let it sit for 5 minutes.

Heat a stainless steel skillet, and brush it lightly with the oil. When the skillet is hot, ladle in ¼ cup of the batter. Cook until bubbles form on the surface, then flip the pancake and cook on the other side 3 to 5 minutes. Repeat with the remaining batter, oiling the pan each time, transferring the finished pancakes to a warm oven until all are done.

MAKES 10 TO 12 PANCAKES

WHOLE GRAINS FOR WHOLE HEALTH

Wheat, spelt, kamut, oats, corn, and rice, unrefined and in their natural state, are among the most nutritionally complete foods. They are a wonderful source of complex carbohydrates, low in fat, and provide good amounts of protein as well as fiber. Refining these grains doesn't make them better; it's strips away the outer bran and germ of the grain, which are the parts that contain most of the nutrients. As with everything we eat, the closer the food is to its live, complete state, the greater its health benefit will be.

Strawberry Whole-Grain Waffles

Whether you choose to top them with sliced strawberries or any other fresh fruit, these tender whole-grain waffles make a truly spectacular breakfast treat.

2	EGGS	1	CUP WHOLE-WHEAT FLOUR
2	CUPS RICE MILK OR ORGANIC MILK, OR MORE AS NEEDED	1	CUP UNBLEACHED WHITE FLOUR
		2	TABLESPOONS RYE FLOUR
2	TABLESPOONS VANILLA EXTRACT	4	TEASPOONS BAKING POWDER
1/3	CUP RAW UNREFINED SUGAR	1/2	TEASPOON GROUND CINNAMON
2	TABLESPOONS TRANS FATS FREE MARGARINE, MELTED	1	CUP THINLY SLICED STRAWBERRIES
		1/2	CUP SAFFLOWER OIL

Preheat the waffle iron according to the manufacturer's instructions. In a large bowl, combine the eggs, rice milk, vanilla, sugar, and margarine. Sift the flours, baking powder, and cinnamon together. Stir the sifted dry ingredients into the egg mixture. If the batter seems too thick, stir in a bit more rice milk. Fold in the sliced strawberries.

Oil the waffle iron and ladle the batter onto the hot iron, leaving a 1-inch border around the edges. Close the iron and cook 3 to 4 minutes, until steam no longer rises from the waffle iron. Remove the waffle and keep it warm in the oven while you make the remaining waffles, re-oiling the iron each time before adding more batter.

MAKES 6 WAFFLES

soups and sandwiches

HEARTY SOUPS, MADE WITH ORGANIC, NUTRIENT-RICH GRAINS, BROTH, AND FRESH VEGETABLES ARE A STAPLE OF THE RANCH DIET. WE SERVE THEM ALMOST DAILY AS A FIRST COURSE AT DINNER OR IN COMBINATION WITH A SANDWICH OR SALAD AT LUNCH.

These soups travel well if you want to pack a school lunch for your ranch hand. A Thermos of Vicky's 5-Onion Bisque (page 82) or Imus Ranch Kids' Favorite Tomato Soup (page 84) with a Fakin' BLT (page 91) or a sandwich we call Wyatt's Favorite Lunch (page 94) and a couple of cookies or brownies for dessert will warm his heart and certainly fill any tummy.

Imus Ranch Kids' Favorite Tomato Soup (page 84)

Broccoli and Cheddar Cheese Soup

Truly creamy and delicious, this velvety soup offers the perfect balance of vegetable and cheese flavors! The soup will keep in the refrigerator, tightly covered in a glass container, for two or three days. Reheat it over a very low flame to avoid scorching.

2	HEADS BROCCOLI, CUT INTO FLORETS	1	CUP GRATED SOY CHEDDAR CHEESE OR SHARP CHEDDAR CHEESE
½	CUP OLIVE OIL		
1	MEDIUM MILD YELLOW ONION, DICED	1	CUP SOY MILK OR ORGANIC MILK
1	CLOVE GARLIC, PEELED AND SLICED THIN	¼	CUP UNBLEACHED WHITE FLOUR
4	CUPS VEGETABLE BROTH	1	TABLESPOON SALT
		½	TEASPOON FRESHLY GROUND BLACK PEPPER

Bring a medium saucepan of water to boil. Add the broccoli, and cook 1 to 2 minutes, until bright green. Rinse the broccoli and drain well. Heat ¼ cup of the oil in a medium stockpot over medium heat. When the oil is shimmering, add the onion and garlic; sauté until tender, about 5 minutes. Combine the onion mixture, broccoli, and half the vegetable broth in the container of a food processor; process until smooth. Add the mixture to the pot and stir in the remainder of the broth; bring to a boil and lower to a simmer. Slowly stir the cheese and soy milk into the soup; continue to simmer 2 to 3 minutes.

Heat the remaining ¼ cup of oil in a sauté pan and stir in the flour. Cook, stirring, until the mixture is smooth and has turned golden brown, about 2 minutes. Stir the flour mixture into the soup just until it is thickened. Add the salt and pepper, adjusting to taste. Remove from the heat immediately and serve.

MAKES 10 SERVINGS

Vicky's 5-Onion Bisque

This thick, rich soup makes a delicious start to just about any meal. That's because each onion lends its own distinct flavor to the mixture—the result is pure harmony. For a creamier soup, add ½ cup soy milk or organic milk with the broth.

¼	CUP OLIVE OIL	2	TABLESPOONS MINCED FRESH THYME, OR
½	MEDIUM RED ONION, SLICED		2 TEASPOONS DRIED
½	MEDIUM WHITE ONION, SLICED	2	TEASPOONS MINCED FRESH DILL, OR
½	BUNCH SCALLIONS, WHITE AND GREEN PARTS,		½ TEASPOON DRIED
	TRIMMED AND SLICED INTO ROUNDS	4	CUPS VEGETABLE BROTH
½	LEEK, WASHED AND DICED	2	TABLESPOONS UNBLEACHED FLOUR
½	CUP DICED SHALLOTS	1	TABLESPOON SALT
10	CLOVES GARLIC, PEELED AND DICED	½	TEASPOON FRESHLY GROUND BLACK PEPPER

Heat 2 tablespoons of the oil in a medium stockpot over medium heat. When the oil is shimmering, add the red and white onions, scallions, leek, shallots, and garlic; sauté, stirring, until the vegetables are tender, about 5 minutes. Transfer the mixture to the container of a food processor and process until smooth. Add the thyme and dill; pulse for 3 seconds. Transfer the puree back to the stockpot, add the broth, and bring to a boil.

While the soup is coming to a boil, heat the remaining 2 tablespoons of oil in a saucepan and, when it is hot, stir in the flour and cook, stirring, until the mixture is smooth and has turned golden brown, about 2 minutes.

As soon as the soup comes to a boil, whisk in the flour mixture until it thickens. Remove from the heat immediately. Add the salt and pepper, adjusting to taste, and serve.

MAKES 6 SERVINGS

Cowboy Potato Chowder

This hearty soup is a particular favorite at the Ranch, so we serve it often for either lunch or dinner (and sometimes both). The kids absolutely love it for its homey and familiar flavors. The soup will keep in the refrigerator in a tightly covered glass container for two or three days. Reheat it over a very low flame to avoid scorching.

½	CUP OLIVE OIL	6	YUKON GOLD POTATOES, PEELED AND DICED
1	MEDIUM ONION, DICED	2	CUPS SOY MILK OR ORGANIC MILK
2	CLOVES GARLIC, PEELED AND DICED	¼	CUP UNBLEACHED WHITE FLOUR
3	TABLESPOONS MINCED FRESH DILL, OR	1	TABLESPOON SALT
	1 TABLESPOON DRIED	½	TEASPOON FRESHLY GROUND BLACK PEPPER
3	TABLESPOONS MINCED FRESH THYME, OR		
	1 TABLESPOON DRIED		
1	14-OUNCE PACKAGE SOY SAUSAGE, CRUMBLED		
4	CUPS VEGETABLE BROTH		

Heat ¼ cup of the olive oil in a medium stockpot over medium heat. When the oil is shimmering, add the onion and garlic; sauté until tender, about 5 minutes. Stir in the dill, thyme, and sausage; cook, stirring, until the sausage is browned, about 5 minutes. Add the broth and potatoes, and bring the soup to a boil. Reduce the heat to medium, cover and simmer about 20 minutes or until the potatoes are tender. Slowly add the soy milk in a steady stream, bring the soup back to the boil, and simmer 2 to 3 minutes.

Heat the remaining ¼ cup of olive oil in a sauté pan. Stir in the flour, and cook, stirring, until the mixture is smooth and light golden brown, about 2 minutes. Whisk the flour mixture into the soup until the soup thickens. Remove from the heat. Add the salt and pepper, adjusting to taste, and serve.

MAKES 10 SERVINGS

Imus Ranch Kids' Favorite Tomato Soup

Don't let the recipe title fool you—this soup definitely isn't only for kids. Grown-ups will love its fresh herb and tomato flavors just as much. The soup will keep in the refrigerator in a tightly covered glass container for two or three days. Reheat it over a very low flame to avoid scorching; if necessary, add a small amount of water to thin it.

¼	CUP OLIVE OIL	1	TABLESPOON MINCED FRESH THYME, OR
½	MEDIUM RED ONION, DICED		1 TEASPOON DRIED
2	CLOVES GARLIC, PEELED AND DICED	1	TABLESPOON MINCED FRESH DILL, OR
1	TEASPOON DRIED ROSEMARY LEAVES, MINCED, OR		1 TEASPOON DRIED
	1 TEASPOON DRIED	8	CUPS VEGETABLE BROTH
3	SPRIGS FRESH SAGE LEAVES, MINCED, OR	4	CUPS VEGETABLE COCKTAIL OR TOMATO JUICE
	1 TEASPOON RUBBED SAGE	1	CUP SOY MILK OR ORGANIC MILK
		3	SPRIGS FRESH BASIL LEAVES, JULIENNED

Heat the oil in a large stockpot over medium heat. When the oil is shimmering, add the onion, garlic, and all the herbs (except the fresh basil), and sauté until the onion is tender, about 5 minutes. Transfer the mixture to the container of a food processor and process until smooth. Return the pureed vegetables to the pot, add the broth and vegetable cocktail, and bring to a boil. Stir in the soy milk, reduce the heat, and simmer 3 to 5 minutes. Remove it from the heat, add the basil, and serve.

MAKES 10 SERVINGS

My Time at the Imus Ranch

MILES GOMEZ

I was really excited when I found out that I was going to the Imus Ranch for the second time. When I got to the hacienda, I saw most everyone I remembered from my first visit: Don, Deirdre, Wyatt, Donnie, and Jack. There were also new people, like Yunk. When the kids all arrived, we were told that we needed to get up early to feed the animals—sheep, horses, goats, and cows—and to get to our chores. It may sound like a lot of work, but it's actually a lot of fun, too.

After a delicious breakfast everyday, we went to the barn to groom and ride the horses, who have a lot of personality. Lunch was sometimes something new to me and always good—my favorite was the Grilled Tofurky Sandwich. In the afternoon, we did a few more farm chores, such as feeding the cattle and checking their water troughs, and weeding and gardening.

Dinner was amazing at the Ranch, and during my second time there, I was able to try even more healthy, tasty food. After suppertime, we went to the dance hall and played hide-and-seek or touch football. At the end of the evening, I went to bed to think of all the good stuff that had happened to me, in spite of one horrible disease—and in that sense, I consider myself lucky.

Tomato-Barley Soup

The secret to this creamy soup is the barley that thickens it, as well as the flour mixture that we add at the end of cooking. In fact, this soup is so thick and luscious, some people have a hard time believing it's made without cream.

¼	CUP OLIVE OIL	2	CUPS VEGETABLE OR TOMATO JUICE
1	ONION, DICED	½	CUP BARLEY, RINSED
1	ZUCCHINI, DICED	3	TABLESPOONS UNBLEACHED WHITE FLOUR
1	RIB CELERY, DICED	1	TABLESPOON SALT
2	CLOVES GARLIC, MINCED	½	TEASPOON FRESHLY GROUND BLACK PEPPER
8	CUPS VEGETABLE BROTH	2	TABLESPOONS MINCED FRESH BASIL

Heat 1 tablespoon of the oil in a large heavy saucepan over medium heat. When the oil is shimmering, add the onion, zucchini, celery, and garlic, and sauté until the vegetables are tender, about 7 minutes.

Transfer the sautéed vegetables to the container of a food processor, add 1 cup of the broth, and process until smooth. Return the mixture to the saucepan, add the remaining 7 cups of broth, the vegetable juice, and the barley. Bring the mixture to a boil, reduce the heat, and simmer, stirring occasionally, about 25 minutes or until the barley is tender.

Heat the remaining 3 tablespoons of oil in a sauté pan, stir in the flour, and cook, stirring, until the mixture is smooth and golden brown, about 2 minutes. Stir the flour mixture into the soup just until it thickens. Remove from the heat immediately. Add the salt and pepper, adjusting to taste. Stir in the basil, and serve.

MAKES 10 SERVINGS

Hot Curried Zucchini Soup

Many zucchini soups are served chilled, but we make this curried version to serve hot. There are many different types of curry powder available; we use a mild red curry, but you can also use a yellow or green variety. Enhanced with the flavors of dill and thyme, this soup is a warm hug on a cool day.

¼	CUP OLIVE OIL		3	TABLESPOON MINCED FRESH DILL, OR
6	MEDIUM ZUCCHINI, DICED			1 TABLESPOON DRIED
½	MEDIUM RED ONION, FINELY DICED		3	TABLESPOON MINCED FRESH THYME, OR
1	RIB CELERY, MINCED			1 TABLESPOON DRIED
2	TABLESPOONS MILD CURRY POWDER		2	CUPS SOY MILK OR ORGANIC MILK
2	CLOVES GARLIC, MINCED		3	TABLESPOONS UNBLEACHED WHITE FLOUR
8	CUPS VEGETABLE BROTH		1	TABLESPOON SALT
			½	TEASPOON FRESHLY GROUND BLACK PEPPER

Heat 1 tablespoon of the oil in a large heavy saucepan over medium heat. When the oil is shimmering, add the zucchini, onion, celery, curry powder, and garlic; sauté until the vegetables are tender, about 10 minutes.

Transfer the sautéed vegetables to the container of a food processor, add 1 cup of the broth, and process until smooth. Return the mixture to the saucepan, add the remaining 7 cups of broth, the dill, and the thyme. Bring the liquid to a boil, reduce the heat, and simmer 15 minutes. Add the soy milk and simmer another 5 minutes.

While the soup is simmering, heat the remaining 3 tablespoons of oil in a sauté pan; stir in the flour, and cook, stirring, until the mixture is smooth and golden brown. Stir the flour mixture into the soup just until it is thickened. Remove from the heat at once. Add the salt and pepper, adjusting to taste, and serve hot.

MAKES 10 SERVINGS

Chicken Jack's 3-Bean Chili

Hearty and flavorful, this recipe is everything you would want in a chili.

1	CUP DRIED BLACK BEANS	1	TABLESPOON CUMIN
½	CUP DRIED SPANISH RED BEANS	1	TABLESPOON CHILI POWDER
½	CUP DRIED ITALIAN WHITE BEANS	1	TABLESPOON MEXICAN OREGANO
2	TABLESPOONS CANOLA OR OLIVE OIL	1	TEASPOON CINNAMON
1	MEDIUM YELLOW ONION, MEDIUM DICE	4	CUPS VEGETABLE BROTH
1	TABLESPOON MINCED GARLIC	4	CUPS WATER
1	JALAPEÑO PEPPER, SEEDS REMOVED, MEDIUM DICE	16	OUNCES FIRE-ROASTED TOMATOES
2	POBLANO PEPPERS, SEEDS REMOVED, MEDIUM DICE	2	TEASPOONS KOSHER SALT
1	RED PEPPER, MEDIUM DICE	1	TEASPOON FRESHLY GROUND BLACK PEPPER

Soak the beans together overnight. Drain. In a large soup pot, heat the oil over medium heat. When the oil is shimmering, add the onion, garlic, and jalapeño, poblano, and red peppers; cook 5 to 10 minutes, until soft.

Add the cumin, chili powder, oregano, and cinnamon; cook, stirring, 1 to 2 minutes. Add beans; stir to evenly distribute seasonings, and add broth and water. Raise heat to high and bring to a boil. Reduce heat to a simmer, leaving the pot uncovered; cook for at least 1 hour or until beans are tender to taste.

Add tomatoes, salt, and pepper; continue simmering for another 20 to 30 minutes, until the chili has thickened. If at any time the liquid falls below the level of the bean mixture, add more broth or water to cover. Adjust salt and pepper to taste.

MAKES 10 SERVINGS

Fakin' BLTs

BLTs have the perfect trio of flavors and textures—the refreshing crunch of lettuce, the crisp and chewy taste of salty-smoky soy bacon, and the tender sweetness of ripe tomatoes. What could be better?

1	TABLESPOON OLIVE OIL	2	TABLESPOONS DIJON MUSTARD
12	TEMPEH BACON STRIPS	8	SLICES SOY CHEDDAR CHEESE OR SHARP
8	SLICES SOURDOUGH BREAD OR FRENCH		CHEDDAR CHEESE
	BAGUETTE	2	PLUM TOMATOES, SLICED
2	TABLESPOONS TRANS FAT FREE MARGARINE	8	LEAVES ROMAINE LETTUCE
8	TABLESPOONS VEGAN OR REGULAR MAYONNAISE		

Heat the oil in a large skillet over medium-high heat. When the oil is shimmering, add the bacon strips and cook until browned, 2 to 3 minutes per side. Remove from pan and set on paper towels to drain.

Spread both sides of each slice of bread with margarine and, using a clean pan, toast 4 to 6 minutes on each side, until golden.

Mix the mayonnaise and mustard together. Spread one side of each slice of bread with 1 tablespoon of the mayonnaise mixture. Top with one slice of cheese, bacon, tomatoes, and lettuce; cover with the remaining bread. Cut in half on the diagonal and serve warm. Repeat for other sandwiches.

MAKES 4 SANDWICHES

Yunk's Grilled Cheese Sandwiches

Paired with a steaming cup of Imus Ranch Kids' Favorite Tomato Soup (page 84), this sandwich sets the stage for a classic American lunch. You may find the cooking method unconventional but, trust me, it tastes great!

8	SLICES WHOLE WHEAT BREAD
	TRANS FAT FREE MARGARINE
4	THICK SLICES SOY AMERICAN-STYLE CHEESE OR
	AMERICAN CHEESE, AT ROOM TEMPERATURE
8	LONG, THIN SLICES CUCUMBER

Spread both sides of each slice of bread generously with margarine. Heat a large stainless steel pan over medium-high heat. When hot, add 4 slices of bread and grill for 1 minute on each side. Remove the grilled bread and immediately cover each with a slice of cheese and 2 slices of cucumber. Grill the remaining 4 slices of bread in the same manner and top the cheese and cucumber with them. The heat from the warm bread will naturally melt the cheese and keep the cucumber crispy.

MAKES 4 SANDWICHES

Egg Salad Sandwiches

These are the tastiest egg salad sandwiches you'll ever eat. Use the freshest organic eggs you can find to ensure the best flavor.

12	EGGS	2	TABLESPOONS PAPRIKA
1	CUP VEGAN OR REGULAR MAYONNAISE		SALT AND FRESHLY GROUND BLACK PEPPER,
½	CUP DIJON MUSTARD		TO TASTE
½	CUP PICKLE RELISH	12	SLICES WHOLE-WHEAT BREAD
½	CUP MINCED SCALLIONS		

Bring a large pot of water to a boil. Add the eggs; allow them to simmer approximately 20 minutes. Drain and run under cold water. Peel the eggs and transfer them to a mixing bowl. Add the remaining ingredients (except the bread) and mash, mixing well.

Toast the bread, spread the egg salad generously on half the slices, cover with the remaining slices, and serve.

MAKES 6 SANDWICHES

Wyatt's Favorite Lunch (Grilled Tofurky Sandwiches)

This sandwich is my son Wyatt's favorite. Made from protein and wheat flour, Tofurky is a delicious vegan product that has all the texture and flavor of turkey. These grilled cheesy sandwiches are perfect by themselves or with a bowl of soup for lunch.

	SAFFLOWER OIL, FOR OILING PAN	3	PLUM TOMATOES, SLICED THIN
1	POUND TOFURKY DELI SLICES	4	SLICES SOY AMERICAN-STYLE CHEESE OR
8	SLICES SOURDOUGH BREAD		AMERICAN CHEESE
¼	CUP TRANS FAT FREE MARGARINE	¼	CUP VEGAN OR REGULAR MAYONNAISE
4	LEAVES ROMAINE LETTUCE	2	TEASPOONS DIJON MUSTARD

Oil a large stainless steel pan with a bit of safflower oil and set it over medium heat. Add the deli slices and cook until brown on both sides, about 3 to 5 minutes. Set the deli slices aside and spread one side of each slice of bread with the margarine. Add half the bread to the pan, buttered side down (work in batches if necessary) and top with the Tofurky, lettuce, tomato, and cheese.

In a small bowl, combine the mayonnaise and mustard, and spread on the unbuttered side of the remaining bread. Top the sandwiches with the second slice of bread so the buttered side is facing up. When the bottom of the bread has browned and the cheese is melting, turn the sandwiches over and brown on the other side. Serve hot.

MAKES 4 SANDWICHES

EDUCATE YOURSELF

DID YOU KNOW THAT . . .

Polyvinyl chloride, found in most of the plastics used to make children's toys, is a toxic chemical that has been linked to brain cancer, leukemia, liver disease, and a number of other debilitating and life-threatening conditions, particularly among small children—who tend to put everything, especially their toys, in their mouth. Simply removing as much plastic as possible from your environment will help to ensure greater health for you and your family.

Take a close look at the labels on children's plastic toys and seek out nontoxic material. Try storing your food in glass rather than plastic containers—the plastic may actually be leaching toxins into your food.

salads and dressings

FRESH FRUITS AND VEGETABLES
ARE AN IMPORTANT PART OF
ANY HEALTHY DIET, AND
FORTUNATELY, ONE OF THE
BEST WAYS TO ENJOY THEM IS
IN A BIG, CRISP SALAD. FULL OF
FIBER AS WELL AS VITAMINS AND
MINERALS, SALADS ARE LIKE A
NUTRITIONAL PLAYGROUND.

Whether it's the refreshing blend of creamy and tart flavors in the Avocado, Raspberry, and Mango Salad (page 100) that cools you on a hot sunny day, or the Spicy Purple Wax Beans (page 102) in a balsamic vinaigrette to accompany a taco or enchilada, or Sidewinder Summertime Coleslaw (page 103) and Perry's Old World Potato Salad (page 110) to go with a veggie burger, you'll be treating yourself to something special when you try any one of the choices in this chapter.

But don't let these recipes limit you. Cruise the aisles of your favorite organic market and see what appeals to you: tender baby spinach leaves? peppery arugula? beautiful bright orange carrots? Pick something new and try it—alone or in combination with something familiar, either with one of our tangy, smooth dressings or with a simple vinaigrette made with extra-virgin olive oil.

Angie's Artichoke and Kalamata Salad

In this salad, the tangy, brine-cured Greek olives add a lot of zip. Serve with a bowl of soup for lunch or as a starter or side dish at dinner.

2	HEADS ROMAINE LETTUCE, WASHED AND TORN	1	CUP PITTED KALAMATA OLIVES
1	BUNCH SPINACH, WASHED AND STEMS REMOVED	3	RIPE MEDIUM TOMATOES, CUT INTO WEDGES
1	CARROT, GRATED	2	CUPS IMUS RANCH SEASONED CROUTONS
1	11.5-OUNCE CAN WATER-PACKED ARTICHOKE		(PAGE 153)
	HEARTS, DRAINED AND TORN INTO PIECES		IMUS HOUSE VINAIGRETTE, TO TASTE (PAGE 121)

Combine the romaine, spinach, and carrot in a large salad bowl. Top with the artichokes and olives, garnish with the tomato wedges and croutons, and pass the vinaigrette on the side.

MAKES 6 SERVINGS

Avocado, Raspberry, and Mango Salad

The smooth avocado, crunchy nuts, and sweet fruits in this salad offer a terrific combination of flavors and textures. For another great variation, try it with our Imus House Vinaigrette (page 121).

4	CUPS MESCLUN SALAD MIX		1	CUP FRESH RASPBERRIES
2	CUPS SPINACH LEAVES		1	MANGO, PEELED AND DICED
2	AVOCADOS, PEELED AND DICED		¼	CUP MR. MARTIN'S MAPLE-GLAZED PECANS
¼	CUP IMUS RANCH HONEY-DIJON DRESSING			(SEE PAGE 148)
	(PAGE 117)			

Combine the mesclun and spinach in a large bowl. Add the avocados and dressing, and toss gently to combine. Transfer to a serving dish and top with the raspberries, mango, and walnuts. Serve with additional dressing on the side, if you like.

MAKES 4 SERVINGS

Spicy Purple Wax Beans

Try this festive bean salad as a side dish with tacos, enchiladas, quesadillas, or veggie burgers—or instead of a regular salad with any meal. We grow gorgeous purple wax beans at the Ranch, but if you can't find them at your grocer, substitute green beans or yellow wax beans and this delicious salad will still be high in vitamins A and C.

1	POUND PURPLE WAX BEANS, TOPPED AND TAILED	3	TABLESPOONS MINCED FRESH OREGANO, OR
½	MEDIUM YELLOW ONION, SLICED VERY THIN		1 TABLESPOON DRIED
½	CUP BALSAMIC VINEGAR	3	TABLESPOONS MINCED FRESH THYME, OR
2	TABLESPOONS CHIPOTLE CHILES IN ADOBO SAUCE		1 TABLESPOON DRIED
1	TEASPOON MINCED GARLIC		SALT AND FRESHLY GROUND BLACK PEPPER, TO TASTE

Bring a medium pot of water to a boil. Add the beans and cook 3 to 5 minutes, until crisp-tender. Drain at once and run under cold water to stop the cooking. Puree the remaining ingredients in the blender to emulsify the dressing, add the beans, toss gently, and refrigerate until ready to serve.

MAKES 4 TO 6 SERVINGS

Sidewinder Summertime Coleslaw

This particular dish is named after one of the trails on the mesa. The kids love the vivid purple color that red cabbage lends to it, but you can use all green cabbage if you prefer. Either way, you're sure to enjoy wonderful results.

3	CUPS SHREDDED RED CABBAGE (½ SMALL)	¼	CUP FRESH LEMON JUICE
3	CUPS SHREDDED GREEN CABBAGE (½ SMALL)	1	CUP VEGAN OR REGULAR MAYONNAISE
1	MEDIUM RED APPLE, CORED AND DICED	2	TABLESPOONS RAW UNREFINED SUGAR
½	CUP RAISINS	1	TEASPOON SALT
¼	CUP SHREDDED CARROTS	½	TEASPOON FRESHLY GROUND BLACK PEPPER

Combine the red and green cabbages, the apple, raisins, and carrots in a large mixing bowl; toss gently with the lemon juice. Fold in mayonnaise until cabbage is well coated, sprinkle with the sugar, season with salt and pepper, and toss again. Chill well before serving.

MAKES 8 SERVINGS

Beets with Balsamic Vinegar

In this dazzling summer-fresh salad, the sweetness of fresh-cooked beets balances perfectly with the tartness of vinegar and lime. If you grow your own beets or buy them with the greens still on, make sure to trim the greens and leave about 1 inch of the stem attached. The greens are delicious in their own right, so save them for another use, such as a quick sauté with olive oil and garlic.

6	MEDIUM BEETS, TRIMMED AND PEELED (ABOUT 1½ POUNDS)	2	TABLESPOONS FRESH LIME JUICE
1	MEDIUM RED ONION, VERY THINLY SLICED	1	TABLESPOON MINCED FRESH OREGANO, OR 1 TEASPOON DRIED
2	TABLESPOONS OLIVE OIL	¼	TEASPOON SALT
2	TABLESPOONS BALSAMIC VINEGAR	¼	TEASPOON FRESHLY GROUND BLACK PEPPER

Fill a medium saucepan with water and heat to boiling. Add the beets and simmer until tender, about 30 minutes. Drain and rinse under cold water. When cooled, cut the beets into ¼-inch-thick slices.

Combine sliced beets, onion, oil, vinegar, lime juice, oregano, salt, and pepper; toss gently. Chill before serving.

MAKES 4 SERVINGS

Mango–Hothouse Cucumber Salad

This hearty but cooling salad is always welcome after a hot morning's work in the New Mexico sun. Once you try it, I'm sure you'll find it's a hit with the kids and adults at your ranch as well. We always use hothouse cucumbers at the Ranch, but any good organic cucumbers will do. The quinoa is a good source of complete protein.

½	HEAD RED LEAF LETTUCE, RINSED AND TORN INTO BITE-SIZE PIECES	½	CARROT, SHREDDED
½	HEAD ROMAINE LETTUCE, RINSED AND TORN INTO BITE-SIZE PIECES	2	TABLESPOONS PREPARED QUINOA (PAGE 206)
3	OUNCES MESCLUN SALAD MIX	1	MANGO, PEELED, PITTED, AND DICED
1	MEDIUM CUCUMBER, PEELED AND SLICED INTO ROUNDS	1	PLUM TOMATO, CUT INTO WEDGES
		1	TABLESPOON SALT
			FRESHLY GROUND BLACK PEPPER, TO TASTE

Combine the lettuces and mesclun in a large salad bowl. In a separate bowl, mix the cucumbers, carrot, and quinoa. Add the vegetables and quinoa to the bowl with the lettuce, and toss to combine. Top with the mango, garnish with the tomato wedges, and season with salt and pepper.

Serve the salad with Imus Ranch Honey-Dijon Dressing (page 117) or Imus House Vinaigrette (page 121).

MAKES 6 SERVINGS

Summer Cool Fruit Salad

There's nothing more refreshing—or good for you—than a bowl of sweet, ripe fruit. This one is as pretty as it is satisfying to eat. If all the fruits aren't available or there are others you prefer, let your imagination inspire your own substitutions.

½	CUP PEELED, PITTED, AND DICED MANGO (1 OR 2 MANGOES)	3	BANANAS, PEELED AND SLICED INTO ROUNDS
1	CUP BLUEBERRIES	3	KIWIS, PEELED AND SLICED
1	CUP RASPBERRIES	1	CUP SEEDLESS GRAPES
1	CUP BLACKBERRIES	½	CUP DRIED, UNSWEETENED COCONUT
1	CUP STEMMED AND SLICED STRAWBERRIES	½	CUP RAW UNREFINED SUGAR

Combine all the fruit in a large decorative bowl and toss well. Sprinkle with the coconut and add the sugar. The sugar will naturally break down to coat the fruit, but feel free to toss the salad until the distribution of colors and flavors is to your liking. Keep refrigerated until ready to serve.

MAKES 6 SERVINGS

Orange-Cashew Spinach Salad

This is a great winter salad that combines the bright color and citrus flavor of oranges with the dark, slightly bitter taste of tender, fresh spinach. The unexpected crunch of roasted cashews is a pleasant surprise.

4	MANDARIN ORANGES	¼	CUP IMUS RANCH HONEY-DIJON DRESSING
1	6-OUNCE-BAG BABY SPINACH LEAVES (ABOUT 6 CUPS)		(PAGE 117)
2	CUPS ROMAINE LETTUCE, RINSED AND TORN	1	CUP ROASTED CASHEWS

Peel and section the mandarin oranges, removing as much of the white pith as possible.

In a large salad bowl, toss together the spinach, romaine, and dressing. Top with the orange sections and sprinkle with the cashews.

MAKES 4 TO 6 SERVINGS

Perry's Old World Potato Salad

This is the best! Nothing beats this classic deli-style potato salad as a side dish with burgers or sandwiches. Just be careful not to overcook or overmix the potatoes, so they won't fall apart.

6	RED POTATOES, PEELED AND CUT INTO 1-INCH CUBES	2	DILL PICKLES, DICED
1	CUP VEGAN OR REGULAR MAYONNAISE	1	TEASPOON TURMERIC
¼	CUP CHOPPED CHIVES	1	TEASPOON SALT
¼	CUP DICED RED ONION	¼	TEASPOON FRESHLY GROUND BLACK PEPPER
¼	CUP DIJON MUSTARD	6	HARD-COOKED EGGS, PEELED AND DICED

Bring a large pot of water to the boil, add the potatoes, and simmer about 12 minutes, until they are just tender. Rinse under cold water to stop the cooking and drain well.

Combine the mayonnaise, chives, onion, mustard, pickles, turmeric, salt, and pepper in a large mixing bowl. Add the potatoes and eggs, and toss very gently until all the ingredients are well coated. Refrigerate and serve cold.

MAKES 8 SERVINGS

EDUCATE YOURSELF

DID YOU KNOW THAT . . .

The March of Dimes recommends taking 400 micrograms of folic acid before and during early pregnancy to help minimize potential defects to the brain and spinal chord of the fetus. Folic acid is a B vitamin found in lentils, leafy green vegetables, broccoli, asparagus, and orange juice. It's difficult to consume enough folic acid from food sources alone, so women—especially those who plan to have children or are pregnant—should consult their physician about taking folic acid supplements.

Vegetable Pasta Salad

Make this pasta salad in the morning and serve it with fresh whole-grain bread for lunch. Better yet, wait and present as a side dish alongside grilled veggie burgers for an informal supper. The flavors blend and intensify with time.

3	CUPS PENNE PASTA		¼	CUP SLICED GREEN SPANISH OLIVES
2	CUPS BROCCOLI FLORETS		½	CUP ROSEMARY-BALSAMIC DRESSING (PAGE 122)
4	PLUM TOMATOES, DICED		3	SCALLIONS, WHITE AND GREEN PARTS CHOPPED
1	CUP DICED RED BELL PEPPER		2	TEASPOONS CHOPPED FRESH ROSEMARY
1	CUP DICED YELLOW BELL PEPPER		½	TEASPOON SALT
¼	CUP SLICED BLACK OLIVES		½	TEASPOON FRESHLY GROUND BLACK PEPPER

Cook the pasta according to package directions and immediately rinse it under cold running water to stop the cooking. Drain well and set it aside.

Steam the broccoli until tender, 5 to 7 minutes, and rinse under cold running water to stop the cooking. Drain well.

In a large bowl, combine the pasta, broccoli, and the remaining ingredients. Toss well to combine, and re-frigerate until serving.

MAKES 6 SERVINGS

Imus Ranch Waldorf Salad

This is our version of a classic—chicken Waldorf salad. Serve it on a bed of lettuce or between two slices of bread for a sandwich. Either way, it makes a filling and nutritious lunch.

FOR THE SALAD

3	CUPS COOKED AND CUBED SOY CHICKEN BREAST
1	APPLE, PEELED, CORED, AND CHOPPED
1	CUP CHOPPED WALNUTS
¼	CUP CHOPPED SCALLIONS
¼	CUP CHOPPED CELERY
⅓	CUP MINCED FLAT-LEAF PARSLEY

FOR THE DRESSING

1	CUP VEGAN OR REGULAR MAYONNAISE
	GRATED ZEST OF 1 LEMON
	JUICE OF 1 LEMON
2	TABLESPOONS MINCED FRESH ROSEMARY
	SALT AND FRESHLY GROUND BLACK PEPPER,
	TO TASTE

Separately combine the salad ingredients and the dressing ingredients. Pour the dressing over the salad, and toss to combine.

MAKES 4 TO 6 SERVINGS

Creamy Caesar Dressing

To create the drama of a classic Caesar salad, break up crisp stalks of romaine lettuce, toss with this dressing, and top with fresh croutons. In this vegan version, the capers offer a nice salty alternative to the traditional anchovy-laced dressing. This dressing will keep for about four days stored tightly covered in the refrigerator.

⅓	CUP BROWN-RICE VINEGAR	1	TABLESPOON LEMON JUICE
½	CUP GRATED RICE PARMESAN CHEESE OR PARMESAN CHEESE	2	CLOVES GARLIC, MASHED
			PINCH OF SALT
⅓	CUP NONPAREIL CAPERS	½	CUP OLIVE OIL
1	EGG OR 2 TABLESPOONS LIQUID EGG SUBSTITUTE	½	CUP SUNFLOWER OR SAFFLOWER OIL

In the container of a food processor, combine all the ingredients except the oils and process 2 to 3 minutes. With the motor running, slowly add the oils through the feed tube until the dressing is thick and blended. If it seems too thick, add a small amount of water to thin it to the consistency you desire.

MAKES 2 TO 2½ CUPS

Creamy Lemon Basil Vinaigrette

From the first whiff, it's clear why lemon basil is so rightly named. In this dressing, the creamy consistency helps the bright citrus flavors cling to each and every leaf. Stash any remaining dressing tightly covered in the refrigerator, where it will keep for about four days.

⅓	CUP BALSAMIC VINEGAR	1	TEASPOON FRESH LEMON JUICE
1	EGG OR 2 TABLESPOONS LIQUID EGG SUBSTITUTE		PINCH OF SEA SALT
¼	CUP PACKED LEMON BASIL LEAVES		PINCH OF BLACK PEPPER
2	TABLESPOONS FRESHLY MINCED FLAT-LEAF PARSLEY	½	CUP OLIVE OIL
		½	CUP SUNFLOWER OR SAFFLOWER OIL

Combine all the ingredients except the oils in the container of a food processor and process 1 to 2 minutes. With the motor running, slowly add the oils through the feed tube until the dressing is thickened and well blended.

MAKES 1 ½ CUPS

Imus Ranch Honey-Dijon Dressing

We use sunflower or safflower oil in many of our dressings because they are monounsaturated—meaning that they help to keep the arteries supple and lubricated—as well as being high in linoleic acid, an essential fatty acid that is one of the major building blocks of the immune system.

¼	CUP HONEY		½	CUP OLIVE OIL
⅓	CUP BALSAMIC VINEGAR		½	CUP SUNFLOWER OR SAFFLOWER OIL
3	TABLESPOONS DIJON MUSTARD		1	TABLESPOON SALT
1	EGG OR 2 TABLESPOONS LIQUID EGG SUBSTITUTE		½	TEASPOON FRESHLY GROUND BLACK PEPPER

Combine the honey, vinegar, mustard, and egg in the container of a food processor and process 1 to 2 minutes. With the motor running, slowly add the oils through the feed tube until the dressing is thickened and well blended. If it seems too thick, add a small amount of water to thin it. Add salt and pepper.

MAKES 1½ CUPS

My Time at the Imus Ranch

CORY FURST

I've never had a better time in my life than I did at the Imus Ranch. And although the whole ranch lifestyle was mostly new to me—something I had only imagined from watching television or reading about the Old West—the whole thing was an amazing experience that made a big difference in the way I think about the earth and my relationship to it.

Deirdre and Don and the other people who work on the Ranch made me feel welcome and comfortable from the moment I arrived at the hacienda. It was also a great opportunity to meet other kids; we worked hard together and also had a wonderful time relaxing and just having fun.

Last but not least, the Ranch has the healthiest, most delicious food that I've ever tasted. In fact, as soon as I got home, I wanted to continue to eat a vegan diet like they serve on the Ranch. So, of course, I wanted all the recipes for the dishes I had while I was there!

BEST FOODS FOR KIDS

**FOODS THAT ARE PARTICULARLY GOOD FOR
GROWING CHILDREN**

Almond butter

Apples

Avocados

Barley

Bok choy

Broccoli

Brown rice

Brussels sprouts

Buckwheat pancakes

Bulghur

Cabbage

Cauliflower

Cocoa

Collard greens

Dates

Eggs

Filtered springwater

Figs

Raspberries

Garlic

Grapefruit

Kale

Lentils

Mustard greens

Oatmeal

Oranges

Parsley

Raw pumpkin seeds

Rye

Soybeans

Spinach

Swiss chard

Vegetable broth

Walnuts

Yogurt

Imus House Vinaigrette

We use many different dressings at the Ranch, but this sweet and fruity one is always a favorite. It will keep for two days stored tightly covered in the refrigerator.

1	CUP FRESH RASPBERRIES	2	TABLESPOONS FRESHLY MINCED FLAT-LEAF PARSLEY
1½	TEASPOONS MINCED FRESH OREGANO, OR ½ TEASPOON DRIED	1	TABLESPOON RAW UNREFINED SUGAR
1½	TEASPOONS MINCED FRESH THYME, OR ½ TEASPOON DRIED	¼	TEASPOON FRESHLY GROUND BLACK PEPPER
		½	CUP RICE VINEGAR
½	TEASPOON MINCED GARLIC	2	CUPS SUNFLOWER OR SAFFLOWER OIL

Combine all the ingredients except the oil in a large bowl. Slowly whisk in the oil until the dressing is thick and well blended.

MAKES 3 CUPS

Imus Ranch Dressing

This wonderfully creamy and herby dressing is the perfect match to just about any salad. And while it may seem like it requires a lot of ingredients, the results are well worth the effort.

½	POUND EXTRA-FIRM SILKEN TOFU, CHILLED IN THE FREEZER FOR AT LEAST 3 HOURS, OR OVERNIGHT	2	RIBS CELERY, FINELY CHOPPED
		½	TEASPOON MINCED GARLIC
½	CUP VEGAN OR REGULAR MAYONNAISE	1	TABLESPOON FRESHLY CHOPPED FLAT-LEAF PARSLEY
¼	CUP LEMON JUICE, OR 2 DROPS ESSENTIAL LEMON OIL	1	TABLESPOON FRESHLY CHOPPED DILL
¼	CUP VEGAN SOUR CREAM OR SOUR CREAM		PINCH OF SEA SALT
1	TEASPOON LOW-SODIUM TAMARI OR SOY SAUCE		PINCH OF FRESHLY GROUND BLACK PEPPER
4	TABLESPOONS FINELY CHOPPED SCALLIONS		TABASCO SAUCE, TO TASTE

Combine all the ingredients in the container of a food processor and blend well for 2 minutes. Serve while still frothy.

MAKES 2 CUPS

Rosemary-Balsamic Dressing

Use your best-quality balsamic in this recipe and even the most ordinary salad will suddenly appear dressed up. The freshest summer herbs are a superb contrast to the rich taste of a well-aged vinegar. This will keep tightly covered in the refrigerator for about four days.

⅓	CUP BALSAMIC VINEGAR	1	TEASPOON FRESH LEMON JUICE
1	EGG OR 2 TABLESPOONS LIQUID EGG SUBSTITUTE		SALT AND FRESHLY GROUND BLACK PEPPER,
2	TABLESPOONS MINCED FRESH ROSEMARY		TO TASTE
2	TABLESPOONS FRESHLY MINCED FLAT-LEAF	½	CUP SUNFLOWER OR SAFFLOWER OIL
	PARSLEY	½	CUP OLIVE OIL

Combine all the ingredients except the oils in the container of a food processor and process 1 to 2 minutes. With the motor running, slowly add the oils through the feed tube until the dressing is thickened and well blended. If necessary, thin the dressing with a small amount of water or additional balsamic vinegar.

MAKES 1 ½ CUPS

Sesame-Soy Vinaigrette

While this dark, nutty dressing will complement just about any ingredient, try putting together an Asian-inspired salad with your favorite sprouts, cucumbers, and radishes mixed into freshly shredded cabbage. This dressing also makes an excellent marinade for tofu, which soaks up all its spicy goodness, or a sauce for whole-wheat buckwheat noodles.

2	TABLESPOONS FRESH LIME JUICE	1	TEASPOON MINCED GARLIC
2	TABLESPOONS SESAME OIL		DASH OF SOY SAUCE
2	TABLESPOONS SESAME SEEDS		DASH OF CIDER VINEGAR
1	TEASPOON GRATED FRESH GINGER	1	CUP OLIVE OIL

Combine all the ingredients except the olive oil in a small bowl. Slowly whisk the oil into the bowl until the dressing is completely blended. Store in the refrigerator until ready to serve.

MAKES 1 1/2 CUPS

Crostini with Olive-Garlic Paté (page 153)

Imus Ranch Barbecue Sauce

In addition to the Imus Ranch Barbecue (page 159), this sauce is delicious slathered on your favorite veggie burger. Its tangy, spicy blend is slightly smoky, thanks to the chipotle chiles in adobo sauce and the fire-roasted tomatoes. This sauce will keep indefinitely if stored in the refrigerator in a tightly covered glass container.

2	TABLESPOONS OLIVE OIL	½	CUP LOW-SODIUM SOY SAUCE
1	MEDIUM RED ONION, DICED	2	TABLESPOONS DRAINED AND MINCED CHIPOTLE
2	CLOVES GARLIC, PEELED AND SLICED		CHILES IN ADOBO SAUCE
1½	CUPS KETCHUP	2	TABLESPOONS FRESHLY BREWED COFFEE
1	28-OUNCE CAN CRUSHED FIRE-ROASTED	1	TABLESPOON TURBINADO SUGAR
	TOMATOES		SALT AND FRESHLY GROUND BLACK PEPPER,
1	CUP FRESHLY SQUEEZED ORANGE JUICE		TO TASTE
½	CUP WORCESTERSHIRE SAUCE		

Heat the oil in a medium saucepan over low heat. When the oil is shimmering, add the onion and garlic, and sauté for 5 minutes, until tender. Stir in all the remaining ingredients, raise the heat to a simmer, and simmer for 45 minutes.

Reheat the sauce with a small amount of water, as it will thicken when it cools.

MAKES 4 CUPS

Cilantro-Dill Sauce

Cilantro, also called Chinese parsley or coriander, is actually a member of the carrot family, and, in fact, its leaves do resemble the fronds of a carrot as well as those of flat-leaf parsley. It's considered a digestive aid and is frequently found in both Mexican and Asian cooking. Use this creamy dressing on salads, tacos, enchiladas, and quesadillas instead of ketchup on your veggie burgers. The sauce will keep tightly covered in the refrigerator for up to a week.

8	OUNCES SILKEN TOFU, DRAINED	3	TABLESPOONS LEMON JUICE
½	CUP CHOPPED CILANTRO		SALT AND FRESHLY GROUND BLACK PEPPER,
1½	TEASPOONS FRESH DILL, OR ½ TEASPOON DRIED		TO TASTE
½	CUP SOY MILK OR ORGANIC MILK		DASH OF TABASCO SAUCE

Combine all the ingredients in the container of a food processor and process until smooth. Transfer to a glass bowl, cover, and refrigerate for at least 1 hour before serving.

MAKES 1¾ CUPS

Lemon-Dill Crabbiless Sauce

This sauce is so good, you shouldn't save it just for Crabbiless Crab Cakes (page 187). Serve it on rounds of crisp toast or use it as a dip for raw vegetables. It's creamy and tangy, but if you choose vegan ingredients it will also be cholesterol-free—so enjoy!

2	CUPS VEGAN OR REGULAR MAYONNAISE	1½	TEASPOONS FRESH DILL, OR ½ TEASPOON DRIED
½	TEASPOON PREPARED WHITE HORSERADISH		DASH OF TABASCO SAUCE
1	TEASPOON FRESH LEMON JUICE	1	TEASPOON GRATED LEMON ZEST

In a small bowl, whisk together all the ingredients and serve.

MAKES 2 CUPS

Imus Ranch Hollandaise Sauce

Use this sauce to dress steamed asparagus, to dip raw vegetables into, or to make classic eggs Benedict. It's guaranteed to transform just about any dish it touches from ordinary to extraordinary.

½	CUP TRANS FATS FREE MARGARINE	¼	CUP FRESH LEMON JUICE
½	CUP RICE MILK OR ORGANIC MILK	1	TEASPOON SALT
5	EGG YOLKS, BEATEN	1	TEASPOON FRESHLY GROUND BLACK PEPPER
1	TABLESPOON AGAR-AGAR, IF NEEDED		

Heat the margarine and rice milk in the top of a double boiler, whisking until creamy, to just below the boiling point. Slowly drizzle in the egg yolks, whisking constantly to prevent them from curdling, and continue whisking until the mixture begins thicken. If necessary, add the agar-agar for additional thickening. Whisk in the lemon juice, salt, and pepper. If the sauce seems too thick, add a dash of hot water to thin it. Serve at once.

MAKES 1½ TO 2 CUPS

Green Onion Cheese Sauce

Nutritional yeast flakes are a pleasant-tasting supplement that's rich in B vitamins and contains the full spectrum of essential amino acids, which are the building blocks of protein. Pour this velvety sauce over steamed cauliflower, broccoli, collard greens, or spinach—yum!

⅓	CUP NUTRITIONAL YEAST	1¾	CUPS RICE MILK OR ORGANIC MILK
¼	CUP MINCED SCALLION	3	CUPS GRATED SOY CHEDDAR CHEESE OR
½	TEASPOON GRANULATED GARLIC		CHEDDAR CHEESE
⅛	TEASPOON DRY MUSTARD		

In a saucepan, combine all the ingredients except the cheese, and bring slowly to a low boil. Gradually stir in the cheese until smooth. If you prefer a thicker sauce, add more cheese.

MAKES 3 CUPS

A WORD ABOUT EGGS

The diet we follow at home and serve at the Ranch would be technically described as organic, whole-food, ovo vegetarian, meaning that we don't eat dairy or animal products, but we do eat eggs. Strictly speaking, a vegan diet would not include eggs because they come from an animal source.

Eggs, however, as long as they are fresh and organic, provide important nutrients including vitamin A, which promotes good vision and healthy bone growth while helping to maintain the integrity of the skin and mucous membranes that function as barriers to bacteria and viruses; vitamin B_{12}, which is necessary for healthy nerve and red blood cells; and vitamin D, which helps to maintain normal blood levels of calcium (necessary for strong bones) and phosphorous. Eggs are one of the few foods that naturally provide the body with vitamin D. They also contain iron and choline, a micronutrient that helps to maintain the structural integrity of the cells and also plays a role in moving fat and cholesterol through the system.

Organic eggs are widely available in supermarkets throughout the country. Those we eat at the Ranch come from our own organically raised chickens, so we can be certain of just how fresh they are and how carefully they're stored. Because of that, we use raw eggs in many of our salad dressings. If you're unsure of the freshness of the eggs you buy or concerned about eating them raw, feel free to use the egg substitutes we suggest in these recipes. Or you can coddle the eggs by cooking them in boiling water for 1 minute before using in a recipe.

Roasted Onion and Garlic Sauce

We serve this creamy gravy with many rice and potato dishes. Because the onions and garlic are slowly baked with the rosemary, their inherent sweetness develops nicely as their flavors intensify.

2	MEDIUM RED ONIONS, PEELED AND CUT INTO WEDGES	2½	CUPS VEGETABLE BROTH
6	CLOVES GARLIC, PEELED	2	TABLESPOONS NUTRITIONAL YEAST FLAKES
1	TABLESPOON CHOPPED FRESH ROSEMARY	2	PINCHES COARSE SEA SALT
⅓	CUP EXTRA-VIRGIN OLIVE OIL	2	PINCHES FRESHLY GROUND BLACK PEPPER
3	TABLESPOONS UNBLEACHED WHITE FLOUR	2	PINCHES FRESHLY GROUND WHITE PEPPER

Preheat the oven to 450°F. Lay a large sheet of unbleached parchment paper in a baking pan. Place the onions and garlic on the paper, sprinkle with the rosemary and the oil, and carefully fold first the long sides and then the short sides of the paper over the vegetables to enclose them completely. Bake 15 to 20 minutes until the onions are soft. (You'll be able to tell this by pressing on the onions through the paper without having to unwrap it.) Remove from the oven, open the paper package, and allow the mixture to cool for a few minutes.

Transfer the vegetables to the container of a blender, add the flour, and blend on high speed for 1 minutes. Add the remaining ingredients and blend 1 more minute. Transfer the sauce to a small saucepan and whisk it over medium heat 5 to 7 minutes, until the consistency of a creamy gravy.

SERVES 6 TO 8

Southwestern Teriyaki Sauce

We use this in stir-fries and as a sauce for Mesa Grande Meatballs (page 162) but you could also spoon it over rice or add it to salad dressing for a special Asian accent.

1¾	CUPS UNDILUTED ORANGE JUICE CONCENTRATE	⅓	CUP HONEY
¾	CUP TURBINADO SUGAR	½	PUREED GUAJILLO CHILE, OR
½	CUP TERIYAKI OR LOW-SODIUM SOY SAUCE		1 TEASPOON CAYENNE PEPPER
½	TABLESPOON GRATED FRESH GINGER, OR		
	1 TABLESPOON GROUND		

Combine all the ingredients in a large bowl and whisk until well blended. This sauce will keep indefinitely if stored tightly covered in the refrigerator.

MAKES 2½ CUPS

Citrus-Tofu Sauce

This is a bright, tart, and creamy sauce that's a perfect topping for sweet dishes such as fruit salad. But because of the nutritional yeast, it works just as well for savory dishes, too. Try this as a topping for enchiladas, quesadillas, or burgers.

12	OUNCES FIRM OR EXTRA-FIRM SILKEN TOFU, DRAINED, OR A 12-OUNCE CONTAINER SOUR CREAM	1	TABLESPOON NUTRITIONAL YEAST
		½	TEASPOON SALT
3	TABLESPOONS FRESH LEMON JUICE OR 3 DROPS ESSENTIAL LEMON OIL (PAGE 55)	2	TEASPOONS WATER, OPTIONAL

Combine all the ingredients in the container of a blender and puree until smooth and creamy.

If the sauce seems too thick, add water to thin. Transfer the mixture to a glass bowl, cover, and chill for 1 hour before serving.

MAKES ABOUT 2 CUPS

Raspberry-Mango Salsa

Serve this fresh salsa with chips or add a dab to a bean burrito for an extra tangy taste. The fire-roasted tomatoes lend a smoky quality that pairs nicely with the bright burst of fruit flavors.

2	CUPS PUREED FIRE-ROASTED TOMATOES	½	CUP DICED MANGO
1	CUP MINCED GREEN ONION	½	CUP DICED RED BELL PEPPER
1	CUP SEEDED AND CHOPPED FRESH PLUM TOMATOES	2	TABLESPOONS MINCED RED ONION
½	CUP WHOLE FRESH RASPBERRIES	2	TABLESPOONS MINCED CILANTRO

In a bowl, gently combine all the ingredients, being careful not to mash to raspberries. Chill for 1 hour to allow the flavors to blend.

MAKES 3 CUPS

Artichoke Dip

Artichokes are high in fiber and virtually fat-free, but preparing them from scratch can be time-consuming. We use chopped artichoke hearts to make this tasty dip to serve with crispy chips, stoned-wheat crackers, or hearty bread.

2	CUPS CHOPPED ARTICHOKE HEARTS
1	CUP GREEN ONION SOUR CREAM (PAGE 144)
1	CUP VEGAN OR REGULAR MAYONNAISE
1	CUP GRATED RICE PARMESAN CHEESE OR PARMESAN CHEESE

1	TEASPOON MINCED GARLIC
	TABASCO SAUCE, TO TASTE
	SALT AND FRESHLY GROUND BLACK PEPPER, TO TASTE

Combine all the ingredients and serve at room temperature.

MAKES 5 CUPS

Cilantro Silk Dip

Use this as a fresh and tangy dip for raw vegetables or tortilla chips. The tofu is a great source of protein, and the herbs are a treat for your taste buds. This sauce will keep indefinitely if stored tightly covered in the refrigerator.

8	OUNCES SILKEN TOFU, DRAINED		2	TABLESPOONS CHOPPED FLAT-LEAF PARSLEY
2	TABLESPOONS VEGAN OR REGULAR MAYONNAISE		1	CLOVE GARLIC, PEELED AND MINCED
2	TABLESPOONS FRESH LEMON JUICE		1	TABLESPOON CHOPPED FRESH DILL, OR
½	CUP CHOPPED CILANTRO			1 TEASPOON DRIED
⅓	CUP DICED SCALLION, GREEN PART ONLY			TABASCO SAUCE, TO TASTE

Combine the tofu, mayonnaise, and lemon juice in a medium bowl and whisk to combine. Stir in the remaining ingredients until thoroughly mixed. Refrigerate, covered, for 1 hour before serving.

MAKES 2 TO 2½ CUPS

Parsley Dipping Oil

At the Ranch, we like to serve this flavorful mixture with bread instead of butter. Be sure to refrigerate it before serving to allow the flavors to blend.

⅔	CUP OLIVE OIL	1	TABLESPOON FRESH LEMON JUICE
5	CLOVES GARLIC, PEELED AND SLICED	½	TEASPOON MUSTARD
1¼	CUP PACKED FLAT-LEAF PARSLEY LEAVES	½	TEASPOON SALT
2	OUNCES SOFT TOFU, DRAINED, OR RICOTTA CHEESE		

Heat the oil in a small saucepan over medium heat. When the oil is shimmering, add the garlic and cook, stirring, until tender but not brown, 8 to 10 minutes. Transfer the garlic and oil mixture to the container of a food processor, add the remaining ingredients, and process until smooth. Refrigerate for 2 hours before serving.

MAKES 1 CUP

New Mexico Red Chili Sauce

Real red chili is made with chile peppers, not a powder. In addition to using this spicy sauce in our Buffalo Red Chili Enchiladas (page 168), this is great over eggs or with pinto beans as a side dish for breakfast. It gets its thickness from the flour and oil combination used at the start of the recipe.

Once it has cooled, the chili can be stored in a tightly covered glass container in the refrigerator for up to one week. To reheat, add a small amount of water (it will thicken when cold) and place it over a very low flame, whisking constantly to avoid scorching.

2 TABLESPOONS OLIVE OIL	1/4 TEASPOON BLACK PEPPER, GROUND
1 SMALL YELLOW ONION, CHOPPED	15 DRIED GUAJILLO CHILES, HALVED, SEEDS
1 TABLESPOON GARLIC, CHOPPED	REMOVED, REHYDRATED FOR 30 MINUTES
1 TEASPOON CUMIN	4 CUPS VEGETABLE STOCK
1 TEASPOON MEXICAN OREGANO	2 TABLESPOONS HONEY
1 TEASPOON KOSHER SALT	

In a 4-quart pot, heat the olive oil over medium heat until hot. When the oil is shimmering, add the onion and garlic; cook for 5 minutes, until soft. Add cumin, oregano, salt, and pepper; continue to cook, stirring for another minute. Add rehydrated chiles, minus the liquid. Stir to distribute the seasonings evenly. Then add the vegetable stock. Raise heat and bring to a rapid simmer. Reduce heat to medium-low and continue cooking for 30 minutes, or until liquid is reduced by half.

Transfer mixture to a blender and pulse until pureed. Add water or more stock for thinning, if necessary. Add honey to the mixture to balance heat. Serve immediately, or transfer back to the pot to rewarm.

MAKES ABOUT 6 CUPS

Eddie's Pico de Gallo

Literally translated from the Spanish, the name for this spicy relish means "rooster's beak." Perhaps it got its name because it's the perfect finger-food sauce, and your thumb and forefinger form a beaklike shape when holding tortilla chips. Once you start into it, it's hard to stop.

5	JALAPEÑO PEPPERS, SEEDED AND MINCED	1	TEASPOON GRANULATED GARLIC
1	MEDIUM WHITE ONION, DICED	1	16-OUNCE CAN CRUSHED TOMATOES, DRAINED
1	TEASPOON SALT	2	TABLESPOONS MINCED CILANTRO

Combine the jalapeños, onion, salt, and garlic; mix well. Mix in the tomatoes, then the cilantro. Taste, and adjust the seasoning with salt and garlic, if necessary.

MAKES ABOUT 2 CUPS

Cowgirl Guacamole

This guacamole is super easy to make. Instead of chopping up all the peppers, onions, and chiles that are used in most guacamole recipes, we begin with our own Imus Ranch Southwest Salsa (page 59). We love our salsa, but you can use any brand you prefer. To prevent darkening, squeeze some fresh lemon juice over the top of the guacamole before covering and refrigerating.

4	RIPE AVOCADOS, PEELED AND SEEDED	½	CUP SALSA
3	TABLESPOONS FRESH LEMON OR LIME JUICE	1	TABLESPOON CHOPPED CILANTRO
4	CLOVES GARLIC, MINCED		SALT, TO TASTE

Combine the avocados, juice, and garlic in a medium bowl; mash with the back of a fork or potato masher. Add the salsa, cilantro, and salt, and mix well to blend flavors. Cover and transfer to refrigerator. Serve cold.

MAKES 4 CUPS

Green Onion Sour Cream

At the Ranch, we use this as a topping for Herbed Twice-Baked Potatoes (page 209) and Edward's Oven-Roasted Potato Skins (page 212) or as a dip for raw vegetables or Imus Ranch Turquoise Buffalo Tortilla Chips (page 59). This will keep indefinitely if stored in a tightly covered glass container in the refrigerator. Do not use an aluminum container for storing this recipe because the acids in the recipe may react with the metal.

1 BUNCH SCALLIONS, WHITE AND GREEN PARTS, RINSED AND TRIMMED	½ POUND FIRM SILKEN TOFU
2 TABLESPOONS OLIVE OIL	2 TABLESPOONS FRESH LEMON JUICE
SALT AND FRESHLY GROUND BLACK PEPPER, TO TASTE	1 TEASPOON RICE VINEGAR
	1 TABLESPOON CHOPPED FRESH DILL, OR 1 TEASPOON DRIED

Preheat the oven to 350°F. Spread the scallions on a sheet pan, coat them with the oil, season with salt and pepper, and roast for 15 minutes. When the onions have cooked, transfer them to the container of a food processor, add the remaining ingredients, and puree until smooth. Taste and season again, if necessary, with salt and pepper.

MAKES 1¼ CUPS

Pimento Cheese

Here's a zippy cheese spread that is so much better than the processed, store-bought versions; the difference is like night and day. It's wonderful on crackers, stuffed into celery sticks, or as a spread for sandwiches. You can forego using a food processor for the preparation of this recipe and the results will be a little less smooth, but delicious nonetheless.

2	CUPS GRATED SOY CHEDDAR CHEESE OR CHEDDAR CHEESE	½	MEDIUM RED BELL PEPPER, FINELY DICED
2	CUPS GRATED SOY MONTEREY JACK CHEESE OR MONTEREY JACK CHEESE	1	CUP VEGAN OR REGULAR MAYONNAISE
		4	TABLESPOONS DIJON MUSTARD
4	RIBS CELERY, FINELY DICED	2	TABLESPOONS SOY SAUCE
4	SCALLIONS, CUT INTO SMALL RINGS	1	TEASPOON SEA SALT
½	MEDIUM RED ONION, FINELY DICED	1	TEASPOON FRESHLY GROUND BLACK PEPPER

Combine the cheeses, celery, scallions, onion, and pepper in a large bowl. In a separate small bowl, use a rubber spatula to combine the mayonnaise, mustard, soy sauce, salt, and pepper to make the dressing. Add the dressing to the cheese and vegetable mixture, folding to combine. Place the pimento cheese in the container of a food processor, and process for 1 minute. Adjust salt and pepper to taste, if necessary.

MAKES 6 CUPS

Salad Bits 'n Bits

These zippy baconless bits add a flavorful crunch to any salad, or you can sprinkle them on Herbed
Twice-Baked Potatoes (page 209). They'll keep indefinitely stored in a covered glass container in the
refrigerator so that you'll always have a batch on hand.

1	CUP WATER		1	TABLESPOON TAMARI OR SOY SAUCE
½	CUP EXTRA-VIRGIN, COLD-PRESSED OLIVE OIL		½	TEASPOON GARLIC POWDER
¼	CUP IMUS RANCH BARBECUE SAUCE (PAGE 127)		¼	TEASPOON ONION POWDER
4	TABLESPOONS MAPLE SYRUP		1¼	CUPS TEXTURED SOY PROTEIN (TSP) GRANULES

Preheat the oven to 350°F. Combine all the ingredients except the TSP in a medium saucepan and bring to a
slow boil. Add the TSP, mix well, and set aside for 10 minutes.

If after 10 minutes the TSP mixture has not absorbed all the liquid, strain it, discard the excess liquid, and
spread the granules on a baking sheet. Bake for 10 minutes. Stir, spread out again, and bake another 10
minutes, until the mixture is lightly browned and slightly crunchy. Cool before serving sprinkled on your
favorite salad.

MAKES 15 TO 20 1-OUNCE SERVINGS

Baked Curried Tofu

Tofu, a complete vegetarian source of protein, is, in effect, the "cheese" made from soy milk. Because it is fairly bland, it will absorb the flavors it's cooked with, which is why it's so good in this curried preparation. We use these spicy tofu nuggets as a condiment, served over Tomato Wehani Rice (page 204), as well as with tacos, enchiladas, and quesadillas.

1	POUND FIRM TOFU, DICED	¾	TEASPOON PAPRIKA
2	TABLESPOONS OLIVE OIL	¾	TEASPOON CURRY POWDER
2	TEASPOONS MINCED GARLIC	¾	TEASPOON DRIED OREGANO
1	TABLESPOON DRIED BASIL	¾	TEASPOON DRIED THYME
1	FRESH GRATED GINGER		SALT AND FRESHLY GROUND BLACK PEPPER, TO TASTE

Preheat the oven to 375°F. In a medium mixing bowl, toss the tofu in the oil until it's evenly coated. Season with the remaining ingredients. Spread the seasoned tofu in a baking dish and bake 30 to 45 minutes, until it is browned. Serve while hot.

MAKES 3 CUPS

Mr. Martin's Maple-Glazed Pecans

Use these crunchy sweet pecans on salads, with desserts, or on stir-fried veggies. You can use the same recipe to make glazed walnuts, as well.

2	CUPS RAW PECANS
½	CUP MAPLE SYRUP
¼	CUP RAW UNREFINED SUGAR
1	TABLESPOON SALT

Preheat the oven to 350°F. Spread the pecans on a baking sheet and toast until lightly browned and fragrant, 8 to 10 minutes. Remove them from the oven and set aside.

Heat the maple syrup and sugar in a medium saucepan over medium heat, stirring frequently, until boiling. Boil the mixture for 2 minutes, and then add the toasted pecans. Continue cooking, stirring to coat the pecans, about 30 seconds more. Spread the pecans onto a baking sheet to cool. Sprinkle with salt.

MAKES 2½ CUPS

Seasoned Tofu with Quinoa

Make up a batch of this savory tofu and serve it over a vegetable sauté or stir-fry. It will help ensure every meal is really tasty and well balanced.

1	TABLESPOON OLIVE OIL			PINCH OF GRANULATED GARLIC
¼	MEDIUM RED ONION, DICED		⅛	TEASPOON GROUND WHITE PEPPER
½	POUND FIRM TOFU, CUBED			PINCH OF PAPRIKA
⅛	TEASPOON CUMIN			SALT, TO TASTE
	PINCH OF GROUND FENNEL SEED		¼	CUP PREPARED QUINOA (SEE PAGE 206)
⅛	TEASPOON CURRY POWDER			

Heat the oil in a large sauté pan over medium heat. When the oil is shimmering, add the onion and sauté about 5 minutes, until tender. Add the tofu, cumin, fennel seed, curry powder, garlic, pepper, paprika, and salt; cook, stirring, 15 to 20 minutes, until the tofu begins to crisp. Add the quinoa and mix well. Serve at once.

MAKES 1 ½ CUPS

Crunchy Munchy Sassy Nuts

These nuts are so good, they're addictive. Keep a bowl on hand for snacking or sprinkle them on ice cream for dessert. They will keep for up to two weeks stored airtight at room temperature.

2	CUPS WHOLE RAW ALMONDS		¾	TEASPOON GROUND CUMIN
2	CUPS RAW PECANS		1	TEASPOON SALT
2	CUPS RAW WALNUT PIECES		1	CUP RAW UNREFINED SUGAR
2	CUPS RAW PUMPKIN SEEDS		½	CUP TRANS FATS FREE MARGARINE
1½	TEASPOONS CAJUN SPICE POWDER		½	CUP MAPLE SYRUP

Preheat the oven to 375°F. Toss the almonds, pecans, walnuts, and pumpkin seeds together in a large bowl and set aside. Combine the spices and salt in a small bowl and set aside.

In a saucepan, combine the nut mixture, sugar, and margarine; heat until the sugar and margarine have melted. Add the maple syrup, stirring to coat the nut mixture evenly. When the mixture begins to bubble, remove it from the heat and spread the nut mixture on a baking sheet. Sprinkle evenly with the reserved spice mixture and toast 10 to 15 minutes, until the nut mixture is caramelized. Remove the pan from the oven, turn the nut mixture, and return to the oven for another 15 to 20 minutes, until the nut mixture appears dry. Remove from the oven and set aside to cool before serving.

MAKES 8 CUPS

My Time at the Imus Ranch

KAWAN GREEN

My visit to the Imus Ranch this past summer was the most awesome and exciting experience of my life. As a city kid born and raised in Passaic, New Jersey, it had certainly never occurred to me that I would be feeding horses, buffalo, longhorns, and sheep and cleaning their stalls and pens—and having an excellent time doing it. The place is a far stretch from what I'm used to at home. Being able to do all my own chores made me feel like a mature and responsible person.

The Ranch is even beautiful at night because the sky is so full of stars. It's amazing to look up and see the constellations and so many stars. One night we even got to see a meteor shower. Small streaks of light fell toward the earth as if they had been dropped like coins. Up in the hills, you can sometimes find tiny pieces of them that actually made it all the way to the surface.

This summer's visit was the third time I have been to the Ranch, and it was really wonderful because Don, Deirdre, Donnie, and the others thought of me as the "old hand." I was able to help teach the other kids the ropes, such as how to mount a horse, how to weed a garden, and even how to herd cattle. On the Ranch, I am just a kid—not a sick or weak kid who needs anything special, just a kid having a great time, being with great people.

Crostini with Olive-Garlic Paté

These tasty, easy-to-prepare crostini make great hors d'oeuvres, or you can spread the paté on crackers for a delicious snack.

1	BAGUETTE	2	TABLESPOONS CHOPPED FRESH SAGE
¼	CUP OLIVE OIL	6	CLOVES GARLIC, PEELED AND SLICED
2	CUPS PITTED BLACK OR GREEN OLIVES	2	TEASPOONS CAPERS
¼	CUP CHOPPED FRESH BASIL		

Preheat the oven to 350°F. Slice the baguette on the diagonal to ½-inch thickness. Place the slices on a baking sheet and toast, turning them once, for about 10 minutes or until crisp.

Heat the oil in medium skillet over low heat. When the oil is shimmering, add the olives, basil, sage, garlic, and capers and cook, stirring, 12 to 15 minutes, or until the garlic is tender. Transfer the mixture to the container of a food processor and process until it is combined and smooth. Transfer to a small bowl and serve with the crostini.

MAKES 1½ CUPS PATÉ

Imus Ranch Seasoned Croutons

Use these in Angie's Artichoke and Kalamata Salad (page 99), in Caesar salad, or in any other salad or soup.

6	SLICES OF SOURDOUGH BREAD, CUT INTO 1-INCH CUBES	1	TABLESPOON DRIED OREGANO
¼	CUP OLIVE OIL	1	TABLESPOON PAPRIKA
1	TABLESPOON DRIED THYME	1	TABLESPOON GRANULATED GARLIC

Preheat the oven to 350°F. In a mixing bowl, combine the bread cubes and the olive oil; toss until all the bread is coated with the oil. Spread the cubes on a baking sheet, sprinkle with the remaining ingredients, and bake 20 to 25 minutes, until the croutons have browned.

MAKES APPROXIMATELY 6 CUPS

Crabbiless Crab Cakes (page 187)

main dishes

IF VEGAN COOKING IS NEW TO YOU, THESE ARE THE RECIPES YOU'LL SURELY BE TURNING TO AGAIN AND AGAIN. THEY ARE THE CENTERPIECES OF THE MEAL, PARTICULARLY AT DINNER, TAKING THE PLACE THAT FISH, MEAT, OR POULTRY MIGHT PREVIOUSLY HAVE HAD AT YOUR TABLE.

I assure you, however, that once you've tried them, you'll never feel deprived. You'll be amazed and delighted by the new variety of flavors and textures coming into your life. You'll probably be eating more than you did, and yet you'll get up from the table feeling lighter, leaner, and more energetic than you thought possible.

Once you become familiar with the products and the cooking methods they require, I hope you'll start inventing dishes of your own and maybe pass them on to me, so we can try them at the Ranch. As I keep saying, learning to live a healthy lifestyle is a continuing journey for me as it is for you, and I'm always eager to learn something new along the way.

Andy's Avocado Burger Melt

These delicious sandwiches are the perfect solution for quick weeknight meals. Store-bought veggie burgers come in so many brands and flavors, you can easily find a lot of variations and never feel as if you've eaten the same burger twice.

2	TABLESPOONS OLIVE OIL		3	OUNCES SOY MONTEREY JACK CHEESE OR
½	MEDIUM RED ONION, THINLY SLICED			MONTEREY JACK CHEESE, SLICED
4	VEGETARIAN BURGERS		3	LARGE PLUM TOMATOES, THINLY SLICED
8	SLICES SOURDOUGH BREAD, TOASTED		1	AVOCADO, THINLY SLICED
2 TO 4	TABLESPOONS DIJON MUSTARD			

Heat the oil in a large skillet over medium-high heat. When the oil is shimmering, add the onion and sauté until tender, about 5 minutes. Remove the onion from the pan, reduce the heat to medium-low, and add the burgers. Cook, turning once, for 8 minutes, or until golden brown. Spread the toast with the mustard. Top four of the toast slices with burgers, then cheese, tomato, avocado, and sautéed onion. Top with the remaining slices of toast, cut in half, and serve warm.

MAKES 4 SANDWICHES

Cajun-Spiced Tofu Burgers

These homemade burgers cook up golden and crunchy on the outside with a slightly spicy, nutty flavor on the inside. Serve them like hamburgers, on buns with ketchup, onion, lettuce, pickles, and mayonnaise . . . all the fixins you like.

2¼	CUPS WALNUTS	1	CARROT, PEELED AND GRATED
1	POUND, 3 OUNCES SILKEN TOFU, DRAINED	1	TEASPOON CAJUN SEASONING
2	CUPS BREAD CRUMBS	¾	TEASPOON SALT
2	RIBS CELERY, FINELY MINCED	3	TABLESPOONS OLIVE OIL

Preheat the oven to 350°F. Spread the walnuts on a baking sheet and toast in the oven until fragrant, about 10 minutes. Remove from pan and set aside to cool. When the nuts have cooled, transfer them to the container of a food processor and pulse until finely ground. Add the tofu, bread crumbs, celery, carrot, seasoning, and salt; process until well combined. Form the mixture into eight ½-inch-thick patties.

Heat the oil in a large skillet over medium heat and cook the burgers, turning them once, until golden on both sides, about 8 minutes.

MAKES 8 SERVINGS

Imus Ranch Barbecue

Make sure there are plenty of napkins around when you serve an Imus-style barbecue because everyone around the table is sure to find it finger-lickin' good!

¼	CUP OLIVE OIL	1	CUP DICED YELLOW SQUASH
2	MEDIUM RED ONIONS, SLICED VERY THIN	1	CUP DICED ZUCCHINI
2	YELLOW BELL PEPPERS, CORED, SEEDED, AND SLICED THIN	1	CUP PLUS 2 TABLESPOONS SEITAN, CUT INTO BITE-SIZE PIECES
2	RED BELL PEPPERS, CORED, SEEDED, AND SLICED THIN	1	CUP IMUS RANCH BARBECUE SAUCE (PAGE 127) SALT AND FRESHLY GROUND BLACK PEPPER, TO TASTE

Heat the oil in a large sauté pan over medium heat. When the oil is shimmering, add the vegetables and sauté, stirring, until they are soft, about 10 minutes. Stir in the seitan and sauté another 3 to 5 minutes, until the seitan is heated through. Stir in the barbecue sauce and simmer on low heat 10 to 15 minutes. Season with salt and pepper, and spoon over your favorite rolls or bread.

MAKES 6 SERVINGS

Cowboy Sloppy Joes

Tomatoey, cheesy, and deliciously drippy, these sloppy sandwiches are a guaranteed favorite with cowboys and cowgirls of all ages.

2	TABLESPOONS OLIVE OIL	½	TEASPOON SALT
1	MEDIUM ONION, DICED	½	TEASPOON FRESHLY GROUND BLACK PEPPER
4	CLOVES GARLIC, PEELED AND SLICED	2	TABLESPOONS WORCESTERSHIRE SAUCE
2	TEASPOONS DRIED OREGANO	1	TEASPOON SPICY MUSTARD (OPTIONAL)
3	TABLESPOONS BALSAMIC VINEGAR	4	CUPS TEXTURED VEGETABLE PROTEIN (TVP)
1	32-OUNCE BOTTLE VEGETABLE COCKTAIL OR TOMATO JUICE	8	WHOLE-GRAIN HAMBURGER BUNS
1	14.5-OUNCE CAN FIRE-ROASTED DICED TOMATOES	2	CUPS SHREDDED SOY MOZZARELLA CHEESE OR MOZZARELLA CHEESE

Preheat the oven to 350°F. Heat the oil in a medium saucepan over medium heat. When the oil is shimmering, add the onion, garlic, and oregano, and sauté until the vegetables are tender, 6 to 8 minutes. Add the balsamic vinegar and boil to reduce by half, about 3 minutes. Add vegetable cocktail, tomatoes, salt, pepper, Worcestershire sauce, and mustard (if using) and bring to a low boil. Simmer for 15 minutes, then add the TVP, and stir until it is thoroughly softened and the liquid is absorbed.

Place the buns on a baking sheet and heat in the oven, turning once, just until warmed through, 4 to 6 minutes. Top the bottom half of each bun with 1 cup of the TVP mixture and sprinkle with ¼ cup of the cheese. Cover with the bun tops and serve immediately.

MAKES 8 SANDWICHES

Mesa Grande Meatballs

Serve these classic Italian favorites with pasta and tomato sauce as a main course, or make them small and put them out on toothpicks with Imus Ranch Barbecue Sauce (page 127) or Southwestern Teriyaki Sauce (page 133) for a delicious hors d'oeuvre.

1	14-OUNCE PACKAGE SOY-BASED SAUSAGE, CRUMBLED	2	TEASPOONS MINCED FRESH GARLIC
½	MEDIUM RED ONION, MINCED	1	TEASPOON FRESH THYME, OR ¼ TEASPOON DRIED
¼	CUP BREAD CRUMBS		DRIED OREGANO, TO TASTE
1	EGG, BEATEN		FRESHLY GROUND BLACK PEPPER, TO TASTE
2	TABLESPOONS KETCHUP	¼	CUP OLIVE OIL

Preheat the oven to 350°F. In a mixing bowl, thoroughly combine all the ingredients except the oil. Pour the oil into a small bowl. Form the sausage mixture into balls and coat them lightly with the oil. Arrange the meatballs in a single layer on a baking sheet and bake for 25 minutes, or until browned.

MAKES 4 SERVINGS

Meatless Meat Loaf

Nothing says "comfort food" like a good old-fashioned meat loaf, and our Ranch version is no exception. If you have any left over, the cold loaf makes great sandwiches, with Imus Ranch Barbecue Sauce (page 127) or just plain ketchup.

2	14-OUNCE PACKAGES SOY GROUND BEEF SUBSTITUTE, CRUMBLED	½	CUP ROLLED OATS
2	EGGS, BEATEN	1½	TEASPOONS DRIED OREGANO
¼	CUP KETCHUP, PLUS EXTRA ¼ CUP (OPTIONAL)	¼	TEASPOON SALT
		¼	TEASPOON FRESHLY GROUND BLACK PEPPER

Preheat the oven to 350°F. In a medium bowl, combine the sausage, eggs, and ketchup; mix well. Add the rest of the ingredients and combine thoroughly with your hands. Form the mixture into a loaf, set it on a baking sheet, spreading remaining ketchup over the top (if desired), and bake for 35 minutes, or until firm and browned.

MAKES 8 SERVINGS

My Time at the Imus Ranch

SHILON WOOTEN

I want to say thank you. Before I came to the Imus Ranch, I thought I wouldn't like it. But it was truly the best experience I've ever had. I would love to go back one day and see Chicken Jack, Yunk, Tracy, Donnie, Matthew, Wyatt, the chefs, Andy and Edward, Jennie, the housekeepers, and everyone else.

SHILON WOOTEN'S MOTHER

Shilon went to the Imus Ranch at the end of August 2003. I had babied Shilon throughout his illness. He had never been away from me, not even just for overnight. But when the invitation came for him to go to New Mexico, my husband simply told me, "Neither one of you has a choice in this. It will be good for him, and he is going." It was difficult for his father and me, but he got on the plane and went.

In one of the Ranch's brochures, the Imuses write that a lot of the kids who visit the ranch have low self-esteem because they have been coddled too much. How true that was! Shilon came home transformed into a different person. He returned with an air of self-confidence that I had never seen. For a week, he did nothing but talk non-stop about his week at the Ranch; he was so proud of himself and what he had done.

In fact, he now wants to become a rancher, just like his idol, Chicken Jack!

I-Man Chimichangas

A chimichanga is really just a burrito sandwich that you pick up and eat with your hands. Serve these with a green salad for a delicious meal. The beans can be cooked in advance and stored tightly covered in the refrigerator for several days.

3	CUPS DRIED PINTO BEANS	½	TEASPOON FRESHLY GROUND BLACK PEPPER
4	CUPS GRATED SOY CHEDDAR CHEESE OR		SALT, TO TASTE
	CHEDDAR CHEESE	2	CUPS SUNFLOWER OIL
1	CUP SALSA	6	8-INCH SPELT FLOUR TORTILLAS
2	TABLESPOONS FRESH LIME JUICE		

Place the beans in a large pot with enough water to cover by 1 inch and bring to a boil over high heat. Turn off the heat and let the pot stand, covered, for 1 hour. Rinse the beans, return to the pot and cover with fresh water; bring to a boil, and cook, stirring often, 1 to 2 hours, until the beans are tender. Drain, mash, and transfer them to a mixing bowl. Add the cheese, salsa, lime juice, pepper, and salt; mix well.

Lay the tortillas on a sheet pan and spread the bean mixture evenly on top, about ¼ inch thick. For each tortilla, fold in the 2 opposite ends, then roll up to form a burrito.

Heat the oil in a large heavy pan. When the oil is shimmering, add the burritos, seam side down. When golden on one side, after about 5 minutes, use tongs to turn them and brown the other side, about 3 to 5 minutes. Do this in batches if necessary, returning the burritos to the sheet pan when they're done. Keep them warm in a 200°F oven.

MAKES 6 CHIMICHANGAS

Southwestern Vegetable and Bean Burritos

If you don't have the time or inclination to soak and cook dried beans for this recipe, you can use one 15-ounce can of pinto beans, rinsed and drained, and the burritos will taste just as good.

1/4	CUP OLIVE OIL	1/8	TEASPOON CUMIN
1/2	CUP RED BELL PEPPERS, SEEDED AND DICED	1/8	TEASPOON OREGANO
1/2	CUP YELLOW BELL PEPPERS, SEEDED AND DICED	1 1/2	CUPS COOKED PINTO BEANS
1/2	CUP PLUM TOMATOES, CORED AND DICED	1 1/2	CUPS SHREDDED SOY MONTEREY JACK CHEESE
1/2	CUP FRESH CILANTRO		OR MONTEREY JACK CHEESE
1	CLOVE GARLIC, MINCED	1/2	TEASPOON SALT
1/2	TEASPOON MEDIUM CHILI POWDER	8	10-INCH SPELT, WHOLE-WHEAT, OR OTHER TORTILLAS

Preheat the oven to 350°F. Heat the oil in a large sauté pan over medium-high heat. When the oil is shimmering, add the peppers, tomatoes, cilantro, garlic, chili powder, cumin, and oregano; sauté until the vegetables are tender, 5 to 7 minutes. Add the beans, 1/2 cup of the cheese, and the salt, and stir to combine.

Heat tortillas, one at a time, in a dry skillet over medium heat, turning them frequently until softened, about 3 minutes total.

Place a tortilla on a flat work surface and spread 1/4 cup of the bean mixture down the center, leaving a 1-inch border at the top and bottom. Sprinkle with 2 tablespoons of the remaining cheese. Fold the top and bottom edges over the mixture and roll up from one side. Carefully transfer the burrito to a baking sheet, seam side down; repeat this process with the remaining tortillas and filling. Transfer the burritos to the oven to warm through, 8 to 10 minutes. Serve warm.

MAKES 8 SERVINGS

Buffalo Red Chili Enchiladas

We have two buffalo on the Ranch and they are the inspiration for this dish—we like to make it using our Imus Ranch Turquoise Buffalo Tortilla Chips (page 59), which are also named after them.

2	CUPS NEW MEXICO RED CHILI SAUCE (PAGE 140)	½	MEDIUM RED ONION, MINCED
1	CUP GRATED SOY CHEDDAR CHEESE OR	1	CUP SHREDDED ROMAINE LETTUCE
	CHEDDAR CHEESE	2	RIPE MEDIUM TOMATOES, CORED AND DICED
5	OUNCES TORTILLA CHIPS, CRUMBLED		

Preheat the oven to 250°F. Combine the chili, cheese, and chips in an ovenproof casserole dish; stir with a spoon until well mixed. Top with the onion and bake 25 to 30 minutes, or until the mixture begins to bubble. Remove from the oven, garnish with the lettuce and tomatoes, and serve hot.

MAKES 4 SERVINGS

Navajo Vegetarian Tacos

This recipe is indigenous to the Southwest and a part of the Navajo culture.

FOR THE BEAN TOPPING

2	CUPS ORGANIC PINTO BEANS, RINSED AND SOAKED OVERNIGHT
1	CLOVE GARLIC, MINCED

FOR THE TACOS

1	HEAD ROMAINE LETTUCE, SHREDDED
4	LARGE TOMATOES, DICED
4	MEDIUM WHITE ONIONS, DICED
1	8-OUNCE PACKAGE SHREDDED SOY CHEDDAR CHEESE OR CHEDDAR CHEESE
1	8-OUNCE PACKAGE SHREDDED SOY JALAPEÑO CHEESE OR JALAPEÑO CHEESE

FOR THE TORTILLAS

3	CUPS UNBLEACHED WHITE FLOUR
1	TEASPOON SALT
2	TEASPOONS BAKING SODA
½	CUP TRANS FAT FREE SPREAD, MELTED
¾	CUP WATER
	SAFFLOWER OIL FOR FRYING (ABOUT 1½ CUPS)

To make the bean topping, drain the beans and place in a medium pot. Add minced garlic and add fresh water to cover by 1 inch. Bring water to boil, and reduce to a simmer. Cook until beans are tender, about 1¼ hours. Drain.

To make the tortillas, combine the flour, salt, and baking soda in a large bowl. Add the melted margarine and water. Stir just until a moist dough forms (it should be stiff enough to hold together). Divide into 6 equal pieces, and roll each piece into an 8-inch round.

In a large skillet, add enough oil to be 1 inch deep. Heat over medium heat until oil is hot. Carefully slip tortillas, one at a time, into the hot oil. The dough will bubble in a few seconds. Cook for about 45 seconds, until slightly browned, and flip to cook the other side, about 15 to 20 seconds until lightly browned. Remove and drain on paper towels. Repeat for remaining tortillas.

To assemble tacos, combine the cooked beans in a medium bowl. Spoon a few tablespoons beans into each taco, and serve with other toppings in separate bowls, so people can create tacos to their taste.

SERVES 6

Ranch Tacos

Seitan is sometimes called wheat meat because it's made from gluten, which is the protein component of wheat with the starch removed. There are recipes for making it from scratch, which is pretty labor-intensive, but luckily you can also buy it ready-made at most health food stores. We love these meaty and cheesy tacos with Imus Ranch Southwest Salsa (page 59).

2	TABLESPOONS OLIVE OIL		SALT, TO TASTE
3	CLOVES GARLIC, PEELED AND MINCED	6	6-INCH FLOUR TORTILLAS
½	MEDIUM RED ONION, FINELY CHOPPED	2	CUPS GRATED SOY CHEDDAR CHEESE OR
4	OUNCES SEITAN, MINCED		CHEDDAR CHEESE
1	TABLESPOON DRIED OREGANO	1	AVOCADO, THINLY SLICED INTO 12 SEGMENTS

Heat 1 tablespoon of the oil in a saucepan over medium heat. When the oil is shimmering, add the garlic and onion and sauté until the onion is tender, about 5 minutes. Add the seitan, season with the oregano and salt, and stir; cook the mixture over medium heat 10 to 15 minutes, until it begins to get crisp.

Brush a large frying pan with some of the remaining oil, add a tortilla, top it with ⅙ of the onion mixture, and sprinkle with ⅙ of the cheese. Add 2 avocado slices to each tortilla. Using a spatula, fold the tortilla over the filling; press down, allowing the cheese to melt. As each taco is done, remove it from the pan and keep warm in a 200°F oven while you continue with the rest of the tortillas, onion mixture, and cheese.

MAKES 6 SERVINGS

Bean Quesadillas

Spelt is one of the most ancient cultivated grains. It's high in fiber and B-complex vitamins, and it contains significantly more protein than wheat. When you're craving a real Southwestern meal, serve these quesadillas with Cowgirl Guacamole (page 142), Spanish Rice (page 203), and chips. We like to use our own Imus Ranch Southwest Salsa (page 59) in this recipe.

2	CUPS DRIED PINTO BEANS (ABOUT 5 CUPS COOKED)	½	CUP OLIVE OIL
		12	LARGE SPELT FLOUR TORTILLAS
2	TEASPOONS MINCED FRESH GARLIC	2	CUPS GRATED SOY CHEDDAR CHEESE OR
2	TEASPOONS DRIED OREGANO		CHEDDAR CHEESE
2	CUPS SALSA		

Rinse the beans, transfer them to a medium stockpot, and add water to cover the beans by 3 or 4 inches. Bring to a boil over high heat, stirring frequently. Reduce heat to a simmer and cook 1½ to 2 hours, until they are soft. If necessary, add more water to keep the beans covered. Drain, transfer the beans to a large mixing bowl, and mash them with a fork. Stir the garlic, oregano, and salsa into the mashed beans.

Heat the oil in a medium frying pan and fry the tortillas 2 to 3 minutes on each side, until they are golden brown and crisp. Spread the bean mixture evenly over half the tortillas, sprinkle with the cheese, and top each with a second tortilla. Cut each quesadilla into 4 wedges and serve 1 whole quesadilla per person.

MAKES 6 SERVINGS

Vicken Quesadillas

Here's another twist on the ever-popular quesadilla—this version uses a soy product that's an excellent imitation of poultry called Veat Chick'n Free Gourmet Bites.

4	TABLESPOONS SAFFLOWER OIL	2	8.5-OUNCE PACKAGES FROZEN VEAT CHICK'N FREE
4	8-INCH WHOLE-WHEAT FLOUR TORTILLAS		GOURMET BITES, THAWED
2	CUPS SHREDDED SOY CHEDDAR CHEESE OR	1	CUP SHREDDED LETTUCE
	CHEDDAR CHEESE	1	TOMATO, DICED

Heat 1 tablespoon oil in a medium skillet. When the oil is shimmering, place one tortilla in the skillet and sprinkle with $\frac{1}{4}$ cup cheese and 2 ounces Gourmet Bites. Use a spatula to fold the tortilla in half, and continue to cook 2 to 3 minutes on each side, until the cheese has melted and the tortilla is browned on both sides. Slide the quesadilla onto a plate and garnish with the shredded lettuce and diced tomato. Repeat with remaining tortillas. Serve warm.

MAKES 4 SERVINGS

Mock Chicken Szechuan Stir-Fry

This dish uses a spicy, dark sauce known to the Szechuan region of western China—it can kick any stir-fry into high gear. You can find prepared Szechuan sauce in the Asian food section of most grocery stores. One other secret of a great stir-fry is to make sure to have all your ingredients chopped and measured before you begin because once you start cooking, this dish comes together fast. This recipe is great served with or without rice.

2	20-OUNCE PACKAGES FROZEN VEAT CHICK'N FREE GOURMET BITES	2	LIMES, HALVED
		3	CARROTS, PEELED AND JULIENNED
1/4	CUP SUNFLOWER OIL	1	HEAD BROCCOLI, CUT INTO SMALL FLORETS
2	TABLESPOONS GARLIC, MINCED	1	CUP FRESH GREEN BEANS, STEMS REMOVED, CUT IN HALF ON A BIAS
2	TABLESPOONS FRESH GINGER, MINCED		
	SALT AND FRESHLY GROUND BLACK PEPPER, TO TASTE	1	CUP BUTTON MUSHROOMS, SLICED
		1	MEDIUM RED BELL PEPPER, CORED, JULIENNED
1/2	CUP SOY SAUCE	3	SCALLIONS, SLICED THINLY ON A BIAS
1/2	CUP SPICY SZECHUAN SAUCE	2	TABLESPOONS WHITE SESAME SEEDS

Defrost the Gourmet Bites by running the plastic pouches under cool water until the pieces begin to separate. Remove from the pouches, place in a bowl, and set aside.

Heat a large sauté pan or wok over medium-high heat. When hot, add 2 tablespoons of the sunflower oil, half the garlic, and half the ginger, and cook for 30 seconds. Add half the Gourmet Bites to the skillet, season with salt and pepper, and sauté for 5 minutes, until lightly browned. Add half of the soy sauce and half of the Szechuan sauce, stir to coat, and cook for 2 minutes, until the sauces are slightly reduced. Transfer from the pan to a large bowl, scraping all the sauce into the bowl. Squeeze a half lime over the mixture, cover with a kitchen towel, and set aside.

Put the sauté pan back on the heat and repeat the entire process using the remaining garlic, ginger, Gourmet Bites, soy sauce, and Szechuan sauce. Add this mixture to the bowl with the other Gourmet Bites mixture and squeeze another half lime over the entire mixture. Cover to keep warm.

Working in batches, sauté the carrots, broccoli, green beans, mushrooms, and red pepper in the remaining 2 tablespoons of sunflower oil; season each lightly with salt and pepper. Sauté each batch no longer than 3 minutes, so that all the vegetables remain slightly crunchy. As you sauté each batch, add it to the large bowl of Gourmet Bites mixture and squeeze some lime juice over it. Keep the bowl covered as you work. When all the vegetables are sautéed, add the raw scallions to the mixture and toss lightly. Garnish with sesame seeds and serve immediately.

MAKES 6 SERVINGS

Mr. Cellophane Sautéed

Cellophane noodles, also known as glass or bean thread noodles, are widely used in Chinese, Thai, and other Asian cuisines. This dish is an Imus Ranch version of an Asian stir-fry.

1	3¾-OUNCE PACKAGE CELLOPHANE NOODLES	3	CLOVES GARLIC, MINCED
¼	CUP OLIVE OIL	¾	CUP ROASTED CASHEWS
1	CUP SLICED CELERY	¼	CUP TAMARI
1	CUP DICED RED BELL PEPPER	3	TABLESPOONS CHOPPED FRESH CILANTRO
1	CUP SNOW PEAS	3	TABLESPOONS CHOPPED FLAT-LEAF PARSLEY
¼	CUP SLICED ONION		

Cook noodles according to package directions. If there are no directions, bring 2 to 3 quarts water to a boil in a medium pot. Turn off the heat, drop the noodles in, and let the pot stand for 15 minutes. Drain the noodles well, toss with 1 tablespoon oil, and set aside.

Heat the remaining 3 tablespoons oil to a large sauté pan or wok over high heat. When the oil is shimmering, add the celery, bell pepper, snow peas, onion, and garlic and sauté until tender, 3 to 4 minutes. Add the noodles. When the noodles are heated, add the cashews and tamari. Toss gently until heated through. Remove from heat and add the cilantro and parsley, tossing again to distribute them evenly throughout the dish.

MAKES 2 MAIN DISH SERVINGS OR 4 APPETIZER SERVINGS

Pasta with Basil-Cilantro Pesto

In addition to this pasta recipe, we also use the basil-cilantro pesto on bread and as a vegetable dip. Try it and I can guarantee you'll be using it often as well. Garnish the dish with a sprig of basil for a hint of the flavor inside.

12	OUNCES CAPPELLINI OR LINGUINE PASTA	2	TABLESPOONS SLICED GREEN ONION
1½	CUPS LOOSELY PACKED BASIL LEAVES	2	TABLESPOONS FRESH LEMON JUICE
1½	CUPS LOOSELY PACKED CILANTRO	1	CLOVE GARLIC
¼	CUP TOASTED PINE NUTS	½	TEASPOON SALT
2	TABLESPOONS TOASTED SUNFLOWER SEEDS	6	TABLESPOONS OLIVE OIL
2	TABLESPOONS GRATED SOY PARMESAN CHEESE OR PARMESAN CHEESE		

Cook pasta according to package directions. Drain and reserve ¼ cup of the cooking water.

Combine the basil, cilantro, pine nuts, sunflower seeds, Parmesan, green onion, lemon juice, garlic, and salt in the container of a food processor and process until roughly chopped. Continue to puree, slowly adding the oil through the feed tube, until the pesto is smooth. Toss the pasta with the pesto and the reserved cooking liquid until well coated. Serve immediately.

MAKES 4 SERVINGS

EDUCATE YOURSELF

DID YOU KNOW THAT . . .

Conventional cotton farmers typically use about ¾ pound of pesticide to grow enough cotton for one pair of denim jeans and ¼ pound of pesticide to grow cotton for one T-shirt? That is not to say wearing jeans or T-shirts is bad. But it is a good idea to stop and count how many pairs of jeans and T-shirts you have in the house right now. Given how much pesticide is leaching into our air, our soil, and our water supply, it's wise to consider buying organic products whenever possible. That way, you will help create a demand for them and thereby reduce the toxicity of our environment.

Penne Primavera with Cream Sauce

The tender-crisp crunch of fresh vegetables adds not only healthy nutrition but also texture to this creamy pasta dish. Serve it with a crisp side salad dressed with our Imus Ranch Vinaigrette (page 121).

1	POUND PENNE PASTA	5	TABLESPOONS CHOPPED FRESH BASIL
2	MEDIUM ZUCCHINI	2	TABLESPOONS CHOPPED FLAT-LEAF PARSLEY
2	YELLOW SUMMER SQUASH	1	TEASPOON GROUND NUTMEG
1/4	CUP OLIVE OIL	1/2	TEASPOON SALT
1	RED ONION, MINCED	1/2	TEASPOON FRESHLY GROUND BLACK PEPPER
3	TABLESPOONS UNBLEACHED WHITE FLOUR	1/4	CUP GRATED SOY PARMESAN CHEESE OR
2	CUPS SOY MILK OR ORGANIC MILK		PARMESAN CHEESE

Cook the pasta according to package directions. While the pasta is cooking, cut the zucchini and yellow squash in half lengthwise and slice into 1/4-inch-thick half-rounds.

Heat 2 tablespoons of the oil in a large saucepan over medium-high heat. When the oil is shimmering, add the zucchini, squash, and onion, and sauté until tender, about 8 minutes. Remove from the pan and set aside.

Heat the remaining 2 tablespoons oil in the same pan, sprinkle with the flour, and cook, whisking constantly, until light golden, 3 to 4 minutes. Stir in the soy milk and continue cooking, whisking constantly, until smooth, thickened, and creamy, about 5 minutes. Stir in the reserved vegetable mixture, the basil, parsley, nutmeg, salt, and pepper, and toss with the cooked pasta. Top with the cheese and serve immediately.

MAKES 6 TO 8 SERVINGS

Grassie's Baked Ziti Casserole

This recipe makes enough so you'll have leftovers to reheat for another meal. The casserole keeps well in the refrigerator for several days, and it's so delicious that you'll be happy to serve it again.

12	OUNCES ZITI	1	TABLESPOON MINCED FRESH SAGE
1	SMALL HEAD BROCCOLI, SEPARATED INTO FLORETS	½	CUP BALSAMIC VINEGAR
1	CUP PEELED AND DICED CARROTS	1	25-OUNCE JAR TOMATO-BASIL SAUCE
2	TABLESPOONS OLIVE OIL	1	CUP CHOPPED ZUCCHINI
1	RED ONION, MINCED	4	CUPS GRATED SOY MOZZARELLA CHEESE OR
1	CLOVE GARLIC, MINCED		MOZZARELLA CHEESE
1	TABLESPOON MINCED FRESH ROSEMARY	¼	CUP GRATED SOY PARMESAN CHEESE OR
2	TABLESPOONS MINCED FRESH BASIL		PARMESAN CHEESE

Preheat the oven to 350°F. Bring a large pot of water to a boil, add the ziti, and boil for 5 minutes. Add the broccoli and carrots; cook 5 to 7 minutes longer, until the pasta and vegetables are tender. Strain the pasta and vegetables and run them under cold water to stop the cooking. Set aside.

Heat the oil in a medium pot over medium heat. When the oil is shimmering, add the onion, garlic, rosemary, basic, and sage and sauté until tender, about 5 minutes. Add the vinegar and boil 1 to 2 minutes to reduce it by half. Add the sauce and when it begins to simmer, add the zucchini and the reserved pasta mixture; stir well.

Transfer the mixture to a 4-quart casserole and add the mozzarella; stir to distribute it evenly throughout. Sprinkle with the Parmesan and bake 35 to 40 minutes, until bubbly. Serve at once.

MAKES 10 TO 12 SERVINGS

Homemade Pizza
with Onion, Bell Peppers, and Olives

A couple of slices of this healthy, low-fat pizza and a small salad makes a great lunch. This pizza even has a cheesy stuffed crust, which is sure to please kids.

3½	CUPS UNBLEACHED WHITE FLOUR	⅓	CUP MINCED FRESH ROSEMARY
⅛	TEASPOON SALT	1	25-OUNCE JAR TOMATO-BASIL SAUCE
1¾	TABLESPOONS QUICK-RISING YEAST	1	RED BELL PEPPER, DICED
1¼	CUPS WARM WATER	1	RED ONION, DICED
⅓	CUP OLIVE OIL	2	CUPS SLICED BLACK OLIVES
1	POUND SOY CHEDDAR CHEESE OR CHEDDAR CHEESE, CUT INTO 4-BY-½-INCH STRIPS	4	CUPS GRATED SOY MOZZARELLA CHEESE OR MOZZARELLA CHEESE

Combine the flour, salt, and yeast in a medium mixing bowl and stir in the water to form a dough. Transfer the dough to a floured surface and knead for about 3 minutes, until it is smooth and elastic. Oil the surface of the dough with a small amount of the olive oil, transfer it to a bowl, cover with a clean cloth, and set it aside in a warm place to rise for 30 minutes. It will rise slightly but will not double in bulk.

Preheat the oven to 375°F. Divide the dough into two equal pieces. Roll each piece into a circle approximately 14 inches in diameter and set them each on a 12-inch pizza pan. Place half the cheese strips around the edge of one pan and roll the dough over the cheese to form a stuffed crust. Repeat with the second crust and the remaining cheese. Brush the dough with a bit more of the olive oil, sprinkle the crusts with the rosemary, and bake them (in 2 batches if necessary) 15 to 20 minutes, until the crust has browned and the cheese is melted.

Remove the crusts from the oven, spread them evenly with the tomato sauce, pepper, onion, olives, and grated mozzarella, and return to the oven for approximately 20 minutes, until the mozzarella has melted and browned. Cut each pie into 8 equal slices and serve hot or at room temperature.

MAKES 16 SLICES

Broccoli and Edamame Casserole

The tender vegetables and rice in this dish are whisked into a luscious cheese-flavored sauce and then covered with a light, flaky crust. As another variation on this casserole, try the Cheesy Cheddar Biscuit dough (page 62) in place of the crust.

FOR THE FILLING

2	MEDIUM POTATOES, PEELED AND DICED
1	CARROT, PEELED AND DICED
2	CUPS VEGETABLE BROTH
1	STALK BROCCOLI, CUT INTO FLORETS
1/3	CUP COOKED WEHANI RICE
1/4	CUP OLIVE OIL, PLUS MORE FOR OILING DISH
1/3	CUP UNBLEACHED WHITE FLOUR
1	CUP FRESH SHELLED EDAMAME
1/2	TEASPOON DRIED THYME
1/4	CUP NUTRITIONAL YEAST FLAKES

FOR THE CRUST

2	CUPS UNBLEACHED WHITE FLOUR
1/8	TEASPOON BAKING SODA
1/8	TEASPOON BAKING POWDER
1/3	TEASPOON SEA SALT
1/3	CUP TRANS FAT FREE MARGARINE
1 TO 2	CUPS SOY MILK OR ORGANIC MILK

Preheat the oven to 350°F. To make the filling, bring a large pot of water to a boil, add the potatoes and carrot, and boil approximately 12 to 15 minutes, until tender. While the potatoes and carrot are cooking, bring the broth to a boil. Add the broccoli and boil 3 to 5 minutes longer. Drain the vegetables and combine them with the cooked rice.

Heat the oil in a sauté pan and whisk in the flour until the mixture is golden brown. Whisk the flour mixture into the boiling broth to form a thick, creamy soup. Oil a 2 ½-quart casserole dish and transfer the potato mixture to it; stir in the edamame, thyme, yeast, and flour mixture.

To make the crust, combine the flour, baking soda, baking powder, and salt in a medium mixing bowl; stir well to combine. With your fingers, work in the margarine until the mixture is crumbly. Add the soy milk slowly just until you can form a soft dough. Knead briefly, and then roll the dough out on a floured surface to a size large enough to cover the casserole.

Cover the casserole with the dough and trim (but do not seal the edges). Bake 30 to 45 minutes, until the crust is brown and flaky.

MAKES 6 TO 8 SERVINGS

Chicken-Less Pot Pie

This chicken-free version of an American classic is chock-full of tender vegetables in a light, creamy gravy. Better yet, it includes a nice flaky crust made with phyllo dough that's sheer tenderness.

4	CUPS BROCCOLI FLORETS		3	TABLESPOONS SAFFLOWER OIL
½	POUND CARROTS, SLICED		¼	CUP UNBLEACHED WHITE FLOUR
24	OUNCES FROZEN EDAMAME BEANS, THAWED		4	CUPS VEGETABLE BROTH
4	8.5-OUNCE PACKAGES FROZEN VEAT CHICK'N FREE NUGGETS, THAWED		8	SHEETS FROZEN PHYLLO DOUGH, THAWED
			1	EGG

Preheat the oven to 350°F. Blanche the broccoli and carrots in boiling water until they are just tender. Transfer the vegetables to a 3- or 4-quart ovenproof casserole, add the edamame and nuggets to the vegetable mixture, and set aside.

To make the gravy, heat the oil in a medium saucepan over medium heat. When the oil is shimmering, add the flour, stirring constantly until the flour turns light brown in color. Whisk the broth into the flour mixture, stirring constantly until it thickens. Pour the gravy into the ovenproof casserole, stirring gently to ensure the nuggets and vegetables are well coated.

Combine the egg with 2 tablespoons water to make an egg wash. Spread a sheet of phyllo dough over the casserole, brush with the egg wash, and then add another sheet of phyllo. Continue adding phyllo and brushing each sheet with egg wash until all the phyllo is used up. Brush the top sheet with the egg wash and bake the casseole 25 to 30 minutes, until golden brown on top.

MAKES 8 SERVINGS

Spicy Bean and Tomato Stew

Kids and cowboys love this served over rice with some crusty bread to sop up the sauce. The black beans, like all legumes, are high in protein as well as fiber, B vitamins, iron, zinc, and complex carbohydrates.

2	TEASPOONS OLIVE OIL	2	LARGE YUKON GOLD POTATOES, PEELED AND DICED
½	CUP DICED YELLOW ONION	2	28-OUNCE CANS FIRE-ROASTED TOMATOES WITH
½	CUP DICED YELLOW BELL PEPPER		JUICE, DICED
1	TABLESPOON DRAINED AND DICED CHIPOTLE	½	CUP COOKED BLACK BEANS
	CHILES IN ADOBO SAUCE	½	CUP COOKED BUTTER BEANS
½	TEASPOON MINCED GARLIC	1	TEASPOON TAMARI
½	TEASPOON DRIED OREGANO	1	TABLESPOON TOMATO PASTE
4	CUPS VEGETABLE BROTH	½	TEASPOON CAJUN SEASONING
			SALT, TO TASTE

Heat the oil in a medium saucepan over medium heat. When the oil is shimmering, add the onions, bell pepper, chipotles, garlic, and oregano and sauté, stirring, 5 to 7 minutes, until the vegetables are tender.

While the vegetables are sautéing, heat the broth in a medium stockpot. When hot, add the potatoes, sautéed vegetables, diced tomatoes, and black and butter beans. Bring to a boil, then lower the heat, and simmer for 20 minutes, until the potatoes are tender. Stir in the tamari, paste, and cajun seasonings and simmer another 20 minutes. Taste the stew and season with the salt. Serve hot.

MAKES 4 TO 6 SERVINGS

Crabbiless Crab Cakes

In addition to the Lemon-Dill Crabbiless Sauce (page 128), we also serve these with Imus Ranch Dressing (page 121). We make our own bread crumbs from sourdough bread from Rudi's Rustic Organic Breads, but you can make your own from any good-quality bread.

2	CUPS GRATED ZUCCHINI	2	TABLESPOONS VEGAN OR REGULAR MAYONNAISE
1	CUP SEASONED BREAD CRUMBS	1	TEASPOON WORCESTERSHIRE SAUCE
¾	CUP GRATED SOY CHEDDAR CHEESE OR CHEDDAR CHEESE	1	TEASPOON DIJON MUSTARD
		½	TEASPOON SALT
½	CUP FINELY DICED RED ONION	½	TEASPOON FRESHLY GROUND BLACK PEPPER
1	EGG, LIGHTLY BEATEN	¼	CUP OLIVE OIL

Combine the zucchini, bread crumbs, cheese, onion, egg, mayonnaise, Worcestershire sauce, mustard, salt, and pepper in a medium bowl; shape the mixture into 6 cakes. Heat the oil in large skillet over medium heat. Add the cakes and cook 7 to 10 minutes on each side, turning once, until golden and cooked through.

MAKES 6 SERVINGS

side dishes

IF YOU ALREADY COOK
VEGETABLES, GRAINS, AND
PASTAS FOR YOURSELF AND
YOUR FAMILY, WHAT I HOPE
YOU'LL DISCOVER IN THIS
CHAPTER IS THE INTENSE
FLAVOR OF ORGANIC
GREENS, THE TEXTURE AND
TASTE OF VARIOUS WHOLE
GRAINS AND RICE, AND THE
ROBUST GOOD HEALTH TO

be gained from eating fresh, live foods grown without pesticides and minimally cooked to preserve their full nutritional value. Beans and broccoli may be old friends, while bok choy and Swiss chard are new ones; perhaps you've cooked with arborio rice but have never tried wehani or basmati. Don't give up your well-known pals, but do take this opportunity to widen your circle. Just as new acquaintances can enrich our social lives in ways we never expected, so widening the variety of foods we eat will enrich our nutrition and add unexpected gastronomic pleasures to every meal.

Herbed Twice-Baked Potatoes (page 209)

Wax Beans Almondine

Almonds are the leading food source of absorbable vitamin E and are widely believed to have significant cholesterol-lowering properties. The almonds lend delicious crunch to the beans. Serve these as a side dish with Meatless Meat Loaf (page 163) or any other main course.

½	CUP SLICED ALMONDS	1	TABLESPOON FRESHLY CHOPPED FLAT-LEAF PARSLEY
3	TABLESPOONS OLIVE OIL	¼	TEASPOON DRIED THYME
¼	MEDIUM RED ONION, DICED		SALT AND FRESHLY GROUND BLACK PEPPER,
1	TABLESPOON MINCED GARLIC		TO TASTE
1	POUND WAX BEANS, TOPPED AND TAILED	¼	CUP FRESHLY SQUEEZED LIME JUICE

Toast the almonds over low heat in a small pan 5 to 7 minutes, just until browned and fragrant. Watch them carefully and shake the pan frequently so they don't burn. When done, remove them from the heat, transfer to a clean towel, and set aside to cool.

Heat the oil in a large sauté pan over medium heat. When the oil is shimmering, add the onion and garlic and sauté about 5 minutes, until tender. Add the beans, parsley, and thyme; sauté until the beans are tender, about 10 to 12 minutes. Season with salt and pepper, sprinkle with the almonds, and serve with the lime juice on the side for an extra splash of flavor.

MAKES 4 TO 6 SERVINGS

Quick Bean and Vegetable Sauté

Kidney beans are a great source of protein and easy to prepare. Here, combined with crunchy, vitamin-rich broccoli, they're also absolutely delicious.

1	HEAD BROCCOLI, CUT INTO FLORETS	1	15-OUNCE CAN KIDNEY BEANS, DRAINED AND
1	TABLESPOON OLIVE OIL		RINSED
½	RED ONION, THINLY SLICED	1 ½	TEASPOONS FRESH DILL, OR ½ TEASPOON DRIED
1	RED BELL PEPPER, SEEDED AND THINLY SLICED	1 ½	TEASPOONS FRESH THYME, OR
1	YELLOW BELL PEPPER, SEEDED AND		½ TEASPOON DRIED
	THINLY SLICED	⅓	CUP VEGETABLE BROTH
1	CLOVE GARLIC, MINCED		FRESHLY GROUND BLACK PEPPER, TO TASTE

Bring a large pot of water to boil and cook the broccoli 1 to 2 minutes, until it is bright green. Drain and immediately run under cold water to stop the cooking and set the color. Set aside.

Heat the oil in a medium saucepan; when the oil is shimmering, add the onion, bell peppers, and garlic, and sauté until the vegetables are tender, about 5 minutes. Add the reserved broccoli, the kidney beans, dill, thyme, and broth, and season with the pepper. Cover and allow the mixture to heat through. Serve at once.

MAKES 4 TO 6 SERVINGS

Zucchini and Summer Squash Sauté

One of the joys of a garden full of zucchini is that there are so many wonderful ways to prepare it. This fast, colorful sauté is one of our favorites.

2	TABLESPOONS SUNFLOWER OIL	2	MEDIUM ZUCCHINI, SLICED INTO ¼-INCH-THICK
½	WHITE ONION, CUT INTO THIN WEDGES		ROUNDS
3	MEDIUM YELLOW SUMMER SQUASH, SLICED INTO	1½	TEASPOONS SALT
	¼-INCH-THICK ROUNDS	½	TEASPOON FRESHLY GROUND BLACK PEPPER

Heat the oil in a sauté pan over medium heat. When it is shimmering, add the onion; sauté until the onion is soft and translucent, about 10 minutes. Add the yellow squash and zucchini and sauté approximately 15 to 20 minutes, until all the vegetables are soft. Season with salt and pepper.

MAKES 4 TO 6 SERVINGS

Bok Choy with Garlic and Sautéed Onions

Also known as Chinese white cabbage, bok choy is a relative of Chinese cabbage; with its crunchy white stalks, it also bears a passing resemblance to wide-stalked celery topped with dark green leaves. This versatile and tasty vegetable dish goes well with almost any main course.

1	HEAD BOK CHOY		1	TEASPOON VEGETABLE-BROTH POWDER
2	TABLESPOONS OLIVE OIL		1	TEASPOON TAMARI
½	MEDIUM RED ONION, DICED		1	TEASPOON LEMON JUICE
4	SMALL CLOVES GARLIC, MINCED		¼	TEASPOON FRESHLY GROUND BLACK PEPPER
¼	CUP WATER			

Slice the bok choy crosswise into 1-inch-thick slices, discarding the tough stems.

Heat the oil in a large skillet over medium heat. When the oil is shimmering, add the onion and garlic, and sauté until the onion is tender, about 5 minutes. Add the bok choy and mix well. In a small bowl, stir together the water, vegetable broth powder, tamari, and lemon juice; add this mixture to the pan. Continue stirring until the bok choy begins to wilt, about 2 to 4 minutes. Season with the pepper and serve hot.

MAKES 4 SERVINGS

Steamed Broccoli with Lemon and Parmesan

In addition to being deliciously simple to prepare, broccoli is also one of the best nutrition choices around. Loaded with fiber, 1 cup of broccoli also provides about 10 percent of the Daily Value for calcium. And in this particular broccoli recipe, the garlic and lemon flavor combination ensures a terrific low-fat side dish that goes well with almost any main course.

4	CUPS BROCCOLI FLORETS	2	TABLESPOONS GRATED SOY PARMESAN CHEESE
2	CLOVES GARLIC, SLICED VERY THIN		OR PARMESAN CHEESE
1	CUP WATER	$\frac{1}{8}$	TEASPOON SALT
2	TEASPOONS FRESH LEMON JUICE		PINCH OF FRESHLY GROUND BLACK PEPPER

Combine the broccoli, garlic, and water in a large sauté pan; bring to a boil. Cover the pan and cook until the broccoli is tender and bright green, 3 to 5 minutes.

Drain, transfer to a serving dish, and sprinkle with the lemon juice, soy Parmesan cheese, salt, and pepper. Serve hot.

MAKES 4 SERVINGS

Tracy's Rainbow Sauté

A relative of the beet family, chard comes in red, green, and our favorite, the rainbow variety, which combines the colors of the two. If it's difficult to find, you can substitute either red or green chard because the three varieties are quite similar in taste. Don't overcook the chard or you'll lose most of its wonderful vitamins and other nutrients.

2	TABLESPOONS OLIVE OIL		$\frac{1}{2}$	CUP WATER
$\frac{1}{4}$	MEDIUM RED ONION, DICED		$\frac{1}{2}$	TEASPOON VEGETABLE-BROTH POWDER
2	CLOVES GARLIC, PEELED AND SLICED			FRESHLY GROUND BLACK PEPPER, TO TASTE
1	BUNCH RAINBOW CHARD, WASHED, STEMMED, AND CHOPPED			

Heat 1 tablespoon of the oil in a large sauté pan over medium heat. When the oil is shimmering, add the onion and garlic; sauté about 5 minutes, until tender. Add the chard and mix well. Add the water, vegetable-broth powder, and the remaining tablespoon of oil. Cover the pan and steam 5 to 7 minutes, until the chard is tender but not wilted. Season with pepper to taste, mix well, and serve.

SERVES 6

Sautéed Yellow Squash with Garlic

One of the most popular of the summer squashes, yellow squash is full of vitamins A and C as well as being moist, juicy, and 100 percent edible, including the seeds and skin. This recipe is quick to put together and pairs nicely with Grassie's Baked Ziti Casserole (page 181).

2	TABLESPOONS OLIVE OIL	¼	CUP WATER
½	MEDIUM RED ONION, DICED	2	TABLESPOONS FRESH LEMON JUICE
4	CLOVES GARLIC, PEELED AND SLICED		SALT AND FRESHLY GROUND BLACK PEPPER,
6	YELLOW SQUASH, CUBED (APPROXIMATELY		TO TASTE
	4 CUPS)		

Heat the oil in a medium-large sauté pan over medium heat. Add the onion and garlic; sauté about 5 minutes, until the onion is tender. Add the squash and water to the pan, cover, and steam 10 to 12 minutes, stirring occasionally, until the squash is tender and easily pierced with a fork. Season with the lemon juice, salt, and pepper. Serve warm.

MAKES 4 TO 6 SERVINGS

Donnie's Baked Vegetable Dumplings
with Miso-Tamari Dipping Sauce

These delicacies are great as either an appetizer or a side dish. They're not hard to make; it just takes a bit of time for the dough to rise. If you like a bit more heat, increase the chipotle chiles to $1/3$ cup.

FOR THE DOUGH

1	PACKAGE ACTIVE DRY YEAST
$1/2$	CUP WARM WATER
1	CUP UNBLEACHED WHITE FLOUR
1	CUP WHOLE-WHEAT FLOUR
2	TABLESPOONS RAW UNREFINED SUGAR
2	TABLESPOONS EXTRA-VIRGIN OLIVE OIL

FOR THE FILLING

2	TABLESPOONS EXTRA-VIRGIN OLIVE OIL
1	TABLESPOON MINCED GARLIC

$1/2$	CUP FINELY DICED YELLOW SQUASH
$1/4$	CUP MINCED CHIPOTLE CHILES
$1/2$	CUP MINCED SCALLION

FOR THE DIPPING SAUCE

1	TABLESPOON RED MISO
1	TABLESPOON RICE VINEGAR
1	TABLESPOON BROWN-RICE VINEGAR
1	TABLESPOON TAMARI
1	TEASPOON HONEY

To make the dough, combine the yeast and water in a large mixing bowl and set aside for 10 minutes or until the yeast is bubbling. Add the flours, sugar, and 1 tablespoon of the olive oil; stir well. Form the mixture into a dough with your hands. If it is too dry, add small amounts of water just until the dough holds together. Transfer the dough to a floured work surface and knead 5 minutes, or until it is smooth and elastic. Add another tablespoon of the oil to the bowl in which you mixed the dough. Turn the kneaded dough in the bowl until it is coated with oil on all sides; cover the bowl with a damp cloth and set it aside to rise in a warm place for 1 hour, or until it has doubled in bulk.

To make the filling, heat the other 2 tablespoons of oil in a stainless steel skillet. When the oil is shimmering, add the garlic and sauté for 1 minute. Add the squash and chipotles and sauté for 2 more minutes. Add the scallion and sauté 2 minutes, or until all the vegetables are tender. Remove from the heat and set aside.

Preheat the oven to 350°F. Punch down the risen dough, form it into a ball, and set it aside for 15 minutes. On a floured surface, roll the dough with your hands into a 12-inch log. Cut the log in half, and then cut each half into 12 equal pieces. Roll 1 piece of dough into a 3-inch circle, place 1 teaspoon of filling in the center of the circle and pull up the edges of the circle to cover the filling, twisting the dough to seal the dumpling. Repeat with the remaining dough and filling, transferring the dumplings to a baking sheet. Bake 10 to 15 minutes, or until the dumplings have browned.

Meanwhile, to make the dipping sauce, stir together the miso, rice vinegars, tamari, and honey in a small bowl. Serve the dumplings hot, with the sauce.

MAKES 24 DUMPLINGS

Asparagus Risotto
with Sun-Dried Tomatoes

In addition to being high in fiber and low in calories, asparagus is one of the best vegetable sources of folic acid, which is necessary for blood-cell formation, growth, and the prevention of liver disease. Serve it simply steamed, with lemon juice and a sprinkling of Parmesan cheese, or in this filling and tasty risotto.

2	TABLESPOONS OLIVE OIL	4	CUPS VEGETABLE BROTH
½	YELLOW ONION, DICED		SALT AND FRESHLY GROUND BLACK PEPPER,
8	SUN-DRIED TOMATOES, SLICED INTO THIN STRIPS		TO TASTE
1½	CUPS ASPARAGUS SLICED DIAGONALLY INTO	½	CUP MINCED FLAT-LEAF PARSLEY
	1-INCH PIECES	¼	CUP GRATED SOY PARMESAN CHEESE OR
1	TEASPOON MINCED GARLIC		PARMESAN CHEESE
2	CUPS (1 POUND) ARBORIO RICE		

In a large saucepan, heat the oil over medium heat. When the oil is shimmering, add the onion, tomatoes, asparagus, and garlic; sauté 3 to 5 minutes, until the vegetables are tender. Add the rice and cook, stirring constantly, until the rice is coated.

Heat the vegetable broth to boiling in a medium pot. Add the rice mixture to the broth, return to a boil, and then reduce to simmer 10 to 15 minutes, until mixture starts to thicken. Cover and simmer 10 to 15 minutes, until the rice is creamy and cooked through. Season with salt and pepper to taste, sprinkle with the parsley and soy or Parmesan cheese, and serve.

MAKES 6 SERVINGS

Basmati Rice
with Chickpeas and Tomatoes

Of the more than 7,000 types of rice in the world, basmati rice is treasured for its distinct nutty flavor and wonderful aroma. Here in this dish, combined with tomatoes and chickpeas, this long-grain variety comes alive. Many kids who've enjoyed it at the Ranch request it often for dinner.

3	CUPS FIRE-ROASTED DICED TOMATOES	2	TABLESPOONS MINCED FRESH FENNEL
1	CUP VEGETABLE BROTH	1½	CUPS BASMATI RICE
2	TABLESPOONS OLIVE OIL	1	15-OUNCE CAN CHICKPEAS, DRAINED AND RINSED
1	CUP DICED RED ONION	1	TABLESPOON SALT
2	CLOVES GARLIC, MINCED	1½	TEASPOONS FRESHLY GROUND BLACK PEPPER

Puree the tomatoes in a food processor and put them in a medium saucepan along with the broth. Set aside.

In a second saucepan, heat the oil over medium heat. When the oil is shimmering, add the onion, garlic, and fennel; sauté until tender, about 4 minutes. Add the rice and chickpeas; sauté 3 to 5 minutes, until the ingredients are browned.

Transfer the rice mixture to the saucepan with the tomatoes, add the salt and pepper, and bring to a boil. Reduce the heat, cover, and cook until the liquid has been absorbed, about 35 minutes. Remove from the heat, fluff the rice with a fork, and serve.

MAKES 6 TO 8 SERVINGS

Brown and Wild Rice Pilaf

This chewy, nutty combination of brown and wild rice makes a pilaf with a pleasing complex texture and taste. Enjoy it with just about any main dish recipe.

6½	CUPS WATER		JUICE OF 1 LEMON
½	CUP WILD RICE	2	CUPS LONG-GRAIN BROWN RICE
2	TABLESPOONS OLIVE OIL	1	TABLESPOON SALT
1	MEDIUM ONION, DICED	½	TEASPOON FRESHLY GROUND BLACK PEPPER
1	CARROT, PEELED AND DICED	1½	CUPS MINCED FLAT-LEAF PARSLEY
1	TABLESPOON TURMERIC		

Bring 3 cups water to a boil in a medium saucepan. Add the wild rice and boil approximately 45 minutes, until the rice puffs and splits. Check periodically and add more water if it becomes completely absorbed before the rice finishes cooking. When done, drain any excess water.

While the wild rice is cooking, heat the oil in a medium sauté pan and add the onion and carrot; sauté about 5 minutes, until the vegetables are tender. Add the turmeric, lemon juice, and brown rice; continue to sauté, stirring, about 5 minutes more, until the rice and vegetables have browned. Add 3½ cups water, salt, and pepper, and bring to a boil; cover, lower the heat, and simmer until the water has been absorbed and the rice is cooked through, 30 to 45 minutes. Add the cooked wild rice to the pilaf and add parsley. Stir well, and serve at once.

MAKES 6 TO 8 SERVINGS

Spanish Rice

Serve this spicy, festive rice for dinner with chili or tacos for a real Southwestern treat. The fire-roasted tomatoes impart a beautifully smoky flavor that complements the different types of chiles in many of our main dishes.

2	TABLESPOONS OLIVE OIL		2	TABLESPOONS DRIED MEXICAN OREGANO
1	CUP LONG-GRAIN BROWN RICE		1	CUP FIRE-ROASTED DICED TOMATOES
1	CUP DICED CELERY		2	CUPS VEGETABLE BROTH
1	CUP DICED ONION			SALT AND FRESHLY GROUND BLACK PEPPER,
1	TEASPOON MINCED FRESH THYME			TO TASTE

Heat the oil in an 8-inch skillet over medium heat. When the oil is shimmering, add the rice, celery, onion, thyme, and oregano, and sauté until lightly browned, approximately 5 minutes. Add the tomatoes and broth, and bring to a boil. Cover, reduce the heat, and simmer until the liquid is absorbed, approximately 25 minutes. Season with salt and pepper to taste, and serve hot.

MAKES 4 TO 6 SERVINGS

Tomato Wehani Rice

This light, aromatic brown rice resembles wild rice when cooked and has an aroma reminiscent of popcorn. Serve this dish with stir-fries or any of the Southwestern enchiladas, tacos, or quesadillas in this book.

3 CUPS WATER OR VEGETABLE BROTH, OR MORE AS NEEDED	1 TABLESPOON DRIED OREGANO
1 CUP WEHANI RICE	DASH OF CUMIN
1 32-OUNCE CAN FIRE-ROASTED TOMATOES	SALT AND FRESHLY GROUND BLACK PEPPER, TO TASTE
1 TABLESPOON MINCED FRESH GARLIC	

Bring the water or broth to a boil in a medium saucepan. Add the rice, lower the heat, and cook covered 20 to 25 minutes, until the rice is cooked through and tender. Check periodically and add more water or broth if it becomes completely absorbed before the rice has finished cooking.

Stir in the tomatoes, garlic, oregano, cumin, salt, and pepper. Serve warm.

MAKES 6 TO 8 SERVINGS

Frances' Vegetable "Fried" Rice

Brown rice takes its name from the outer bran coating that is left intact rather than removed in milling, as it is in white rice. Because of this, it is higher in fiber, vitamin B, and important minerals than white rice is. It also takes a while longer to cook, but the delicious nutty flavor, as well as the additional nutritional value, make it worth the time. The edamame in this dish also provides a good source of protein.

3	TABLESPOONS OLIVE OIL, DIVIDED	3	CUPS WATER
1	CUP LONG-GRAIN BROWN RICE	2	EGGS, LIGHTLY BEATEN
3	CARROTS, PEELED AND DICED	1	CUP SHELLED FRESH EDAMAME, STEAMED UNTIL
½	MEDIUM RED ONION, DICED		TENDER; OR FROZEN EDAMAME, THAWED
3	TABLESPOONS TAMARI		FRESHLY GROUND BLACK PEPPER, TO TASTE

Heat 2 tablespoons of the olive oil in a medium saucepan. When the oil is shimmering, add the rice, carrots, onion, and 2 tablespoons of the tamari; cook, stirring constantly, until the rice is browned and the vegetables are tender, approximately 5 to 8 minutes. Add the water and bring to a boil. Reduce the heat, cover, and cook until the rice is cooked through and the water had been absorbed, approximately 40 minutes.

When the rice is done, heat the remaining tablespoon oil in a small skillet over medium heat. Cook the eggs as you would scrambled eggs, stirring gently as they set and tossing in the remaining tablespoon tamari 1 minute or so before they're done. Fold the eggs and edamame gently into the rice mixture, and season with pepper to taste. Transfer the rice to a serving bowl, and fluff with a fork.

MAKES 4 SERVINGS

Quinoa

Quinoa, an ancient grain from the Andes Mountains, is a complete protein with an almost ideal balance of essential amino acids, which is why it has been called the perfect protein. Make sure to rinse the quinoa carefully before cooking or it can have a bitter, soaplike taste. Once prepared, it will keep for several days stored in an airtight container in the refrigerator, at the ready for several recipes.

3	CUPS WATER
1½	CUPS QUINOA, RINSED AND DRAINED

Bring the water to a boil in a medium saucepan over medium heat. Add the quinoa, cover, and simmer 25 to 30 minutes, until the water is absorbed and the quinoa is tender. Remove from the heat, fluff with a fork, and let stand for 5 minutes. Cooked quinoa can be used in other recipes such as the one below.

MAKES 5½ CUPS

Raspberry-Quinoa Applesauce

This is a great side dish to serve either at breakfast or as a side dish with Meatless Meat Loaf (page 163).

1	POUND RED APPLES	1	TEASPOON GROUND CINNAMON
1	CUP PREPARED QUINOA (ABOVE)	1 TO 2	TEASPOONS FRESHLY GRATED NUTMEG
½	CUP RASPBERRY-BANANA PUREE (PAGE 240)	¼	TEASPOON GROUND ALLSPICE
2	TABLESPOONS RAW UNREFINED SUGAR		

Bring a large pot of water to a boil. While the water is coming to a boil, peel, core, and slice the apples. When the water is boiling, add the apples and cook until soft, about 10 minutes. Drain and transfer the apples to the container of a food processor. Add the remaining ingredients and process until smooth. The applesauce is equally good served warm or cold.

MAKES 2 CUPS

Apple and Pear Quinoa Compote

Serve this as a sweet and delicious, protein-packed side dish for either lunch or dinner.

¼	CUP GOLDEN RAISINS	1	TEASPOON CINNAMON
2	TEASPOONS MAPLE SYRUP	1	GRANNY SMITH APPLE, PEELED AND CHOPPED
⅓	CUP UNCOOKED QUINOA	1	GREEN PEAR (SUCH AS ANJOU), PEELED AND CHOPPED
⅔	CUP WATER		
½	TEASPOON VANILLA EXTRACT	¼	TEASPOON SALT
2	TABLESPOONS RAW UNREFINED SUGAR		

Place the raisins in a small bowl, drizzle them with the maple syrup, and set aside. Rinse the quinoa well in cold water and place it in a saucepan along with the water, vanilla, sugar, and cinnamon. Add the raisins and bring the mixture to a boil over medium heat. When boiling, add the apple, pear, and salt; cover, reduce the heat, and simmer 15 to 20 minutes, until the liquid is absorbed. Serve warm or at room temperature.

MAKES 4 TO 6 SERVINGS

PUT HEALTHY COLOR IN YOUR LIFE WITH VEGETABLES

• Green vegetables are an important source of calcium.

• Almost one-third of the calories broccoli offers are from protein.

• Dark green leafy vegetables are an excellent source of the dietary fiber that regulates blood sugar and cholesterol levels as well as bowel function, while animal products contain none.

• The best source of vitamin A, which is essential for good vision and bone growth, is in the beta-carotene found in carrots, pumpkins, sweet potatoes, and dark green vegetables such as broccoli, spinach, chard, collards, kale, and mustard greens.

• Vitamin K is essential for blood coagulation. It is manufactured by the friendly bacteria that naturally live in our bodies, but some experts believe that it can be destroyed by taking antibiotics or eating products from factory-raised animals. Green leafy vegetables are an excellent source of vitamin K.

• The deeper the color, the greater the gain. Pale green vegetables such as iceberg lettuce, celery, and cucumbers contain mainly water with some fiber and provide virtually no nutrition. That's one of the reasons they're often on the "unlimited" lists of diet foods. Enjoy them, but don't count on them to provide healthy nutrients. Our greenhouse at the Ranch is a blaze of color, which signifies an abundance of health.

Herbed Twice-Baked Potatoes

Too many of us have come to think of potatoes as fattening when, in fact, they are not only fat-free but rich in vitamins C and B6, as well as potassium and dietary fiber. Half a potato served with a nice big salad makes a great lunch or light supper. A quarter of a potato per person is the perfect portion to serve as a side dish for a heartier meal.

3	LARGE IDAHO POTATOES	1	CUP GRATED SOY CHEDDAR CHEESE OR
3	TABLESPOONS OLIVE OIL		CHEDDAR CHEESE
	SALT AND FRESHLY GROUND BLACK PEPPER,	¼	CUP TRANS FATS FREE MARGARINE
	TO TASTE	¼	CUP SALAD BITS 'N BITS (PAGE 146)
¼	CUP SNIPPED CHIVES	1	CUP GREEN ONION SOUR CREAM
2	TABLESPOONS DRAINED AND FINELY MINCED		(PAGE 144)
	CHIPOTLE CHILES IN ADOBO SAUCE		

Preheat the oven to 375°F. Wash the potatoes, coat them with the olive oil, season with salt and pepper, and bake 45 minutes to 1 hour, until they are easily pricked with a fork. Remove from the oven and, when the potatoes are cool enough to handle, slice them in half and carefully scoop out the flesh without damaging the skins. Set the skins aside and transfer the flesh to a bowl. Add the chives, chipotles, half of the soy cheese, the margarine, and Salad Bits 'n Bits. Mash and stir with a fork until the ingredients are well combined; carefully return the mixture to the potato skins, dividing it equally among them. Sprinkle each serving with some of the remaining cheddar, and return the potatoes to the oven for about 5 minutes to melt the cheese. To serve, top each potato with a dollop of sour cream.

MAKES 6 SERVINGS AS A LUNCH OR LIGHT DINNER, OR 12 SERVINGS AS A SIDE DISH

Ranch-Style Herbed Potatoes

Yukon gold potatoes derive the first part of their name from the fact that they were developed by the potato-breeding program at the University of Guelph in Canada and the second part from their buttery-flavored golden flesh. We serve these with almost anything, from a stir-fry to Mesa Grande Meatballs (page 162), veggie burgers, or Meatless Meat Loaf (page 163), for either lunch or dinner.

5	POUNDS YUKON GOLD POTATOES, SCRUBBED WELL, SKIN ON, CUT INTO 2-INCH CUBES	1/3	CUP CHOPPED FLAT-LEAF PARSLEY
1/3	CUP EXTRA-VIRGIN OLIVE OIL	1	TEASPOON DRIED OREGANO
2	CUPS DICED RED ONION	1	TEASPOON DRIED THYME
1	CUP DICED SHALLOTS	1/2	TEASPOON SALT
2	TABLESPOONS MINCED GARLIC	1/4	TEASPOON FRESHLY GROUND BLACK PEPPER

Bring the potatoes to a boil in a large pot of water. While the potatoes are boiling, heat the oil in a large skillet. When the oil is shimmering, add the onion, shallots, and garlic; sauté 5 to 7 minutes, until tender and browned. When the potatoes are tender, after about 20 to 25 minutes, drain and add them to the pan with the onion mixture. Season with the remaining ingredients and cook, tossing, 20 to 25 minutes, until the potatoes have browned.

MAKES 6 TO 8 SERVINGS

Ranch Rosemary Scalloped Potatoes

Serve these with Meatless Meat Loaf (page 163) and a green vegetable for a real comfort-food dinner.
We use a terra-cotta casserole dish for these, but you can also use a glass baking dish.

2	TABLESPOONS OLIVE OIL	2	TABLESPOONS NUTRITIONAL YEAST FLAKES
4	CUPS RED SKIN OR FINGERLING POTATOES,		SALT AND FRESHLY GROUND BLACK PEPPER, TO TASTE
	SCRUBBED WELL, SKIN ON, THINLY SLICED	1¼	CUPS SOY MILK OR ORGANIC MILK
½	CUP FINELY CHOPPED RED ONION	1	TABLESPOON CHOPPED FRESH ROSEMARY

Preheat the oven to 400°F. Oil a 2-quart casserole dish with 1 tablespoon of the oil.

Spread 1 cup of the potatoes in the bottom of the casserole and sprinkle with 2 tablespoons of the chopped onion and ½ tablespoon of the yeast flakes. Season lightly with salt and pepper. Continue layering the casserole in this way until all the potatoes, onion, and yeast flakes are used. Sprinkle with the remaining tablespoon of oil, pour the soy milk over all, and scatter the rosemary over the top. Bake 45 minutes to 1 hour, or until the potatoes are tender and easily pierced with a fork.

SERVES 4 TO 6

Edward's Oven-Roasted Potato Skins

At the Ranch, we use the scooped-out potato flesh leftover from this dish to make hash browns for breakfast. You can do the same by simply seasoning the potato with salt and pepper, forming it into patties, and frying them in olive oil until golden.

4	MEDIUM BAKING POTATOES, SCRUBBED WELL	½	CUP COOKED AND CRUMBLED SOY SAUSAGE OR SOY BACON
3	TABLESPOONS OLIVE OIL, PLUS MORE FOR OILING THE POTATOES	1	TEASPOON PAPRIKA
2	CUPS SHREDDED SOY CHEDDAR CHEESE OR CHEDDAR CHEESE	2	TABLESPOONS MINCED CHIVES, FOR GARNISH

Preheat the oven to 400°F. Lightly rub potatoes with oil, place them on a baking sheet, and bake until tender, 45 to 55 minutes. Set aside, and when they are cool, cut them in half lengthwise and scoop out the flesh, leaving a ¼- to ½-inch-thick shell. Cut each potato skin into 4 wedges and place them on the baking sheet in a single layer. Drizzle with the oil, and top with the cheese and sausage. Raise the oven to 450°F and bake the skins approximately 15 minutes, until they are golden and the cheese has melted. Sprinkle with the paprika and chives just before serving.

MAKES 6 TO 8 SERVINGS

My Time at the Imus Ranch

DAEVIN KIRSCHNER

When I was given the chance to go the Imus Ranch, from the moment I stepped off the airplane, I knew that I was very lucky. The green and brown terrain was beautiful, and the dry, warm air was fresh. When I arrived at the Ranch's hacienda, I was amazed at the size of it. Soon after the other kids and I had met Don and Deirdre, we were given Western boots, jeans, shirts, and even cowboy hats. I was surprised that I looked normal in them, as if I'd been wearing them all my life.

Properly suited up, we were ready to be cowboys and cowgirls. We started the day nice and early, and we soon learned the routine: every morning, feeding the animals and doing ranch chores; in the afternoon, riding horses.

The horse I rode every day was named Cody. One day he wasn't well, so I rode Woody instead, a specially trained animal who listens extra carefully. We rode mostly around the Ranch, but one day we went into the hills nearby to look for Indian arrowheads and potsherds. That day we actually found a cute puppy! We had to figure out how best to get him back to take care of him.

One of my favorite things was going for a dip in the Ranch's swimming hole—it felt good to be cooled down in the heat. At night, we went to the pool hall, where there's also a jukebox. It was like a big party, and even if you didn't know how to shoot pool or dance, there were board games to play—definitely something for everyone.

Don does his show in the pool hall in the mornings, and my best day was when I went on his program. At first I was a little nervous. But Don was easy to talk with, and after I started talking into the mic, I relaxed. The Imus Ranch is the coolest place that I've been to!

Fresh Coconut Cake (page 218)

desserts, sweet sauces, and beverages

DESSERT IS AN IMPORTANT PLEASURE AND A SWEET WAY TO END A GOOD MEAL. THAT'S WHY ADOPTING A HEALTHIER DIET DOESN'T AUTOMATICALLY MEAN YOU SHOULD GIVE UP DESSERT.

Instead, try these nutritious and equally sweet alternatives to the preservatives and trans fats that accompany most store-bought cookies, cakes, and ice creams. Our Buckin' Bronco Brownies (page 220), for example, are as chewy and rich as any you've ever tried. My Favorite Strudel (page 231) will remind you of the warm fruit flavors wafting from your grandmother's kitchen—if you were lucky enough to have a grandma who baked a strudel as good as this one! No-Bake Chocolate Oatmeal Cookies (page 221) are a cinch to make and great to have on hand for an afternoon snack. And Ranch Banana Splits (page 234) are just as wonderful as those from any ice cream parlor. Even the shakes and smoothies easily pass for dessert—in liquid form. Enjoy them all!

Chocolate Bundt Cake

This lovely cake is simple to make and delicious enough to serve just as is, but it can also be topped with a scoop of nondairy vanilla ice cream or yogurt. If there's any left over, you can store it, covered airtight, at room temperature for several days.

	SAFFLOWER OR SUNFLOWER OIL, FOR OILING PAN	$\frac{1}{8}$	TEASPOON SALT
$1\frac{3}{4}$	CUPS UNBLEACHED WHITE FLOUR, PLUS MORE FOR DUSTING PAN	$\frac{1}{2}$	CUP TRANS FATS FREE MARGARINE
		$1\frac{1}{2}$	TABLESPOONS RICE MILK OR ORGANIC MILK
$\frac{1}{2}$	CUP UNSWEETENED COCOA POWDER	1	TEASPOON VANILLA EXTRACT
$1\frac{2}{3}$	CUPS RAW UNREFINED SUGAR	$\frac{1}{4}$	CUP WATER
$1\frac{3}{4}$	TEASPOONS BAKING SODA	2	EGGS

Preheat the oven to 350°F. Lightly oil the inside of a 12-cup Bundt pan and dust it lightly with flour, shaking out the excess.

Combine the flour, cocoa, sugar, baking soda, and salt in the bowl of an electric mixer; mix well with a fork. In a separate bowl, combine the margarine, milk, vanilla, water, and eggs; whisk until the mixture is creamy. Add the wet ingredients to the flour mixture and beat on medium speed, frequently scraping down the sides of the bowl, for 4 minutes. Pour the batter into the prepared pan and bake 30 to 40 minutes, until a toothpick inserted in the center comes out clean. Let the cake cool completely in its pan before turning it out onto a serving platter.

MAKES 12 SERVINGS

Carrot Cake

Rich in vitamin A, beta-carotene, and phytochemicals, carrots are a nutrition powerhouse that help boost the immune system and fight off infection. Baked in this moist, dense cake, of course, they are also naturally sweet and delicious. Since this cake is dense, a small slice will satisfy, but it will also stay moist and fresh for several days if covered airtight and stored at room temperature.

	SUNFLOWER OR SAFFLOWER OIL, FOR OILING PAN	1¾	CUPS RAW UNREFINED SUGAR
2	CUPS UNBLEACHED WHITE FLOUR	1	TEASPOON VANILLA EXTRACT
1	TEASPOON BAKING SODA	1	CUP OLIVE OIL
1	TEASPOON BAKING POWDER	2	CUPS FINELY GRATED CARROTS
½	TEASPOON SALT	1	CUP CHOPPED WALNUTS
4	EGGS		

Preheat the oven to 350°F. Oil an 8-inch or 9-inch springform pan.

Sift together the flour, baking soda, baking powder, and salt; set aside. In the bowl of an electric mixer, combine the eggs, sugar, and vanilla; beat until light and fluffy. Add the oil and beat just to combine. Add the carrots and walnuts to the egg mixture and stir well.

Add the wet ingredients to the flour mixture and beat well to combine. Pour the batter into the prepared pan and bake 1 to 1¼ hours, or until a toothpick inserted in the center comes out clean. Cool in the pan before removing the sides.

MAKES 12 SERVINGS

Fresh Coconut Cake

This cake is a little bit of light, delicious heaven with the pleasant surprise of strawberries tucked between the layers. You can also use ¹/₂ cup cleaned and hulled strawberries mixed with ¹/₂ cup of strawberry spread for the filling.

	OLIVE OIL, FOR OILING PANS	1¹/₄	CUP RICE MILK OR ORGANIC MILK
1	CUP SAFFLOWER OIL	1	TEASPOON VANILLA EXTRACT
2	CUPS RAW UNREFINED SUGAR	1	CUP EGG WHITES (ABOUT 8 LARGE EGGS,
4	EGG YOLKS (RESERVE WHITES FOR BATTER)		INCLUDING RESERVED WHITES)
2¹/₄	CUPS UNBLEACHED WHITE FLOUR	1	CUP STRAWBERRIES, CLEANED AND HULLED
1	TEASPOON SALT	1	CUP WHIPPED TOFU TOPPING (PAGE 236)
4	TEASPOONS BAKING POWDER	1	CUP FRESH GRATED COCONUT, FOR GARNISH

Preheat the oven to 350°F. Oil two 9-inch cake pans with olive oil.

In the bowl of an electric mixer, cream the safflower oil and sugar together on high speed until fluffy. Beat in the egg yolks one at a time. In another bowl, sift the flour, salt, and baking powder together; add the flour mixture to the egg mixture, and stir in the milk. Mix well on medium speed, about 3 to 4 minutes; stir in the vanilla. In a clean, dry bowl, beat the egg whites into soft peaks, and gently fold them into the batter. Pour into the pans and bake for 30 to 35 minutes, or until a toothpick inserted into the center comes out clean. Remove the cake from the oven and allow it to cool completely. Remove and slice each cake horizontally to make 4 layers total.

Meanwhile, put the strawberries in a blender and blend about 1 minute to make a puree. Lay one cake layer on a cake dish, and spread a third of the strawberry puree on top; repeat with two other layers and the rest of the puree. Add the final layer to the top, and cover with the whipped tofu topping. Garnish with the grated coconut. Transfer to the refrigerator and chill for 30 minutes before serving.

SERVES 12

My Time at the Imus Ranch

DAEVIN KIRSCHNER'S MOTHER

My son, Daevin, was a normal healthy boy until the age of 13. Then, on March 31, 1999, the unthinkable happened. Daevin went for an MRI, and the results showed he had a brain tumor and a cyst. That same night he was operated on, and we were told that the surgeon removed all the cancer and that Daevin would lead a healthy and normal life.

But the tumor came back, and he underwent three more operations.

In August 2000, Daevin was invited to visit the Imus Ranch. He had had his final surgery and radiation and was still recovering, but he wanted to go to the Ranch more than anything. His first night at the hacienda, he had a seizure. The Imus Ranch had a nurse stay with him until he felt better.

At the Ranch, he was treated like a normal child and received no preferential treatment because of his illness. He did his chores like the other kids, and he had his own horse that he took care of. He told me that the best time he had was when Deirdre took the group riding. He deeply loved the Ranch and the Imus family and wanted to work at the Ranch the following summer.

I will never forget when he came home, wearing a cowboy hat and boots walking up the stairs. I opened the door, and he said, "Howdy, Mama."

At that moment, I knew that in those 10 days at the Ranch, my son had changed: He had made the transition from being a boy to being a man.

On March 7, 2001, we lost our Daevin at the age of 16. He was one of those people who touched you with his lust for life and his gift to make people laugh.

The Imus Ranch is a truly amazing resource for children like Daevin. I will forever be grateful that Daevin had the opportunity to visit the Imus Ranch.

Buckin' Bronco Brownies

Anyone who likes chocolate surely loves brownies. And this particular recipe serves up enough dense, luscious treats for a whole crowd of chocolate lovers to enjoy. These are hands-down rich, chewy, and scrumptious. Store the brownies in an airtight container.

¾	CUP UNBLEACHED WHITE FLOUR	⅓	CUP TRANS FATS FREE MARGARINE, AT ROOM TEMPERATURE
¼	CUP WHOLE-WHEAT OR RYE FLOUR		
1	CUP RAW UNREFINED SUGAR	2	EGGS
½	CUP COCOA POWDER	2	TEASPOONS VANILLA EXTRACT
½	TEASPOON BAKING SODA	¼	CUP VEGAN CHOCOLATE CHIPS OR SEMI-SWEET CHIPS
½	TEASPOON BAKING POWDER		
¼	TEASPOON CINNAMON	3	PACKAGES DARK CHOCOLATE BUG BITES, CHOPPED

Preheat the oven to 325°F. In a large mixing bowl, stir together the flours, sugar, cocoa, baking soda, baking powder, and cinnamon. Stir in the margarine until the mixture resembles coarse crumbs. Stir in the eggs and vanilla. Fold in the chocolate chips and a third of the Bug Bites and stir to combine and distribute the ingredients.

Spread three-quarters of the mixture evenly in a 9-by-13-inch pan lined with unbleached parchment paper; scatter the remaining Bug Bites over the top and use the rest of the batter to cover them with a thin layer. Bake approximately 20 minutes, or until a toothpick inserted in the center comes out clean. Remove from the oven and cool in the pan. When cool, cut into 2-inch squares.

MAKES 16 BROWNIES

Gingersnap Cookies

Typical gingersnap recipes usually call for adding molasses to the mix. But in this version, the use of all-natural ingredients means that the light flavor of molasses is already present in the raw unrefined sugar. What you have left is a cookie delicately spiced with ginger, cinnamon, and cloves—these are sure to be better than any commercial gingersnaps you've ever tasted.

4	CUPS UNBLEACHED WHITE FLOUR		2	CUPS RAW UNREFINED SUGAR
1	TABLESPOON GROUND GINGER		2	EGGS
1½	TEASPOONS BAKING SODA		½	CUP MAPLE SYRUP
1	TEASPOON GROUND CINNAMON		2	TEASPOONS APPLE-CIDER VINEGAR
½	TEASPOON GROUND CLOVES		1	TEASPOON WATER
¾	CUP TRANS FATS FREE MARGARINE			

Sift together the flour, ginger, baking soda, cinnamon, and cloves. In a separate bowl, using an electric mixer, beat together the margarine, sugar, and eggs until light and fluffy. Stir in the syrup, vinegar, and water. Slowly add dry ingredients to the wet until blended. Refrigerate the dough for 2 hours.

Preheat the oven to 350°F. With floured hands, roll the dough into 1½ inch balls, place them on a baking sheet, and flatten them to ⅓ inch thick. Bake 10 to 12 minutes, or until golden brown. Cool on the baking sheet before serving.

MAKES 4 DOZEN COOKIES

No-Bake Chocolate Oatmeal Cookies

These chewy chocolate treats are nutty and sweet and easy to make—the perfect cookie to make when your ranch hands want to help out in the kitchen.

1	CUP RAW UNREFINED SUGAR	¼	CUP ALMOND BUTTER
¼	CUP RICE MILK OR ORGANIC MILK	½	TEASPOON VANILLA EXTRACT
¼	CUP TRANS FATS FREE MARGARINE		PINCH OF SALT
2	TABLESPOONS UNSWEETENED COCOA	2	CUPS QUICK-COOKING OATS

Line a baking sheet with unbleached parchment paper and set aside. Heat the sugar, milk, margarine, and cocoa in a medium saucepan over medium heat, stirring until well blended. Boil for 1 minute. Remove from the heat and add the almond butter, vanilla, and salt. Stir in the oats and mix well to blend. Spoon in heaping-teaspoon portions onto the prepared baking sheet and refrigerate for 2 hours before serving.

MAKES 2½ DOZEN COOKIES

Walnut-Chocolate Chip Cookies

Remember the classic Toll House cookie from childhood? While it probably conjures up many warm memories, this version is even better because it's loaded with more nutrients. You'll benefit from a touch of fiber from the oatmeal and the vitamin E in the walnuts. It's not quite like a vitamin pill, but every little bit helps!

1½	CUP UNBLEACHED WHITE FLOUR	1½	TEASPOONS VANILLA EXTRACT
¾	TEASPOON BAKING POWDER	1	EGG
½	TEASPOON SALT	1	CUP ROLLED OATS
¾	CUP TRANS FATS FREE MARGARINE	¾	CUP CHOCOLATE CHIPS
¾	CUP RAW UNREFINED SUGAR	¾	CUP CHOPPED WALNUTS

Preheat the oven to 375°F. Sift together the flour, baking powder, and salt. In the bowl of an electric mixer, combine the margarine, sugar, and vanilla; beat on medium speed for 2 minutes, or until creamy. Add the egg and continue beating until the mixture is glossy, about 1 minute more. Stir the flour mixture into the margarine mixture until well blended. Then stir in the oats, chocolate chips, and walnuts.

Drop the batter by rounded tablespoons onto a cookie sheet 2 inches apart. Flatten the cookies with floured fingers and bake 10 to 12 minutes, or until golden. Remove from the pan and cool on a rack.

MAKES 2½ DOZEN

Arborio Sweet Rice Pudding

Arborio is a short-grain Italian rice that contains a higher percentage of soluble starch than regular long-grain rice. It's the starch that gives arborio its characteristic creaminess, which makes it ideal not only for risottos but also for this creamy, raisin-studded pudding. It will keep, tightly covered in the refrigerator, for several days, but it's really best eaten right away!

¾	CUP ARBORIO RICE	2	TABLESPOONS RAW UNREFINED SUGAR
2	CUPS WATER	1	CUP RAISINS
1¾	TABLESPOONS VANILLA EXTRACT	2	CUPS RICE MILK OR ORGANIC MILK
1	TABLESPOON HONEY	¼	TEASPOON GROUND CINNAMON

Bring the rice and 1 cup of the water to a boil in a medium saucepan. Reduce the heat to a simmer. Add the remaining water ¼ cup at a time and stir until liquid is absorbed. Add the vanilla, honey, and sugar. Cook over medium heat just until the honey and sugar have liquefied and the mixture is hot. Add the raisins and stir to distribute them throughout the rice. Stir in the rice milk. Continue simmering until the milk is just absorbed. Remove from heat. Spoon the rice into 6 individual serving dishes, sprinkle each portion with a dash of cinnamon, and serve. Or, if you prefer, refrigerate the pudding and serve it cold.

MAKES 6 SERVINGS

BLUE MOON TREATS

The reason diets don't usually work is that they're mostly all about deprivation, and that's not the way I choose to live my life. Rather, I believe we all need to treat ourselves well to avoid feeling deprived, so I strongly recommend that you enjoy a good treat from time to time. Think about eating something you really love, even if you know it is truly junky or unhealthy. My own favorite treat is M&Ms. Don would probably say that his is a really great hot dog. Yours might be a big, sticky, fluffy glazed doughnut or a bag of potato chips. In our family, we call these "blue moon treats" because we indulge only rarely—or, once in a blue moon. Whatever your treat is, make sure it's something you're sure to enjoy and save it for self-indulgence once in a great while. Then, when you do indulge, enjoy every single bite and don't even <u>think</u> of feeling guilty.

Buckley's Lemon Meringue Tart

The fresh sunny flavor of lemon, the melt-in-your-mouth froth of meringue, and the flakiness of a tender crust—all three elements of this luscious tart combine perfectly to make this a truly spectacular dessert.

FOR THE CRUST

SAFFLOWER OR SUNFLOWER OIL, FOR OILING PAN

1⅓ CUPS UNBLEACHED WHITE FLOUR, PLUS MORE FOR FLOURING PAN

½   TEASPOON SEA SALT

2   TEASPOONS RAW UNREFINED SUGAR

½   CUP TRANS FATS FREE MARGARINE

2 TO 4 TABLESPOONS COLD WATER

1   TEASPOON BROWN RICE VINEGAR

FOR THE FILLING

¾   CUP RAW UNREFINED SUGAR

2   TABLESPOONS ARROWROOT

2   TABLESPOONS UNBLEACHED FLOUR

1   TEASPOON KOSHER OR SEA SALT

1½ CUPS WATER

ZEST OF 2 LEMONS (ABOUT 1 TABLESPOON)

⅓   CUP FRESH LEMON JUICE

4   EGG YOLKS

1½ TABLESPOONS TRANS FATS FREE MARGARINE

FOR THE MERINGUE

½   CUP RAW UNREFINED SUGAR

3   TABLESPOONS WATER

6   EGG WHITES

½   TEASPOON CREAM OF TARTAR

Preheat the oven to 350°F. Oil and flour a 9-inch tart pan.

To make the crust, combine flour, salt, and sugar; stir until blended. Cut in margarine until mixture forms coarse crumbs. In a bowl, combine the water and vinegar; add this mixture slowly to flour mixture, stirring just until a dough forms. Press into a ball and flatten into a thick disk. Sprinkle a clean surface with a little flour and roll out dough to an 11-inch circle. Transfer dough to the tart pan, prick several times on bottom with a fork, and allow dough to settle. Bake 15 to 20 minutes, just until crust starts to darken. Do not turn off the oven.

To make the filling, combine the sugar, arrowroot, flour, salt, and water in a saucepan; bring the mixture to a boil over medium heat, stirring constantly. Lower heat and simmer the mixture 1 to 2 minutes, until thickened. In a bowl, combine lemon zest, juice, and yolks. Add lemon mixture to filling; stir in margarine. Cook 3 more minutes. The filling will continue to thicken. Remove filling from heat, pour into the prebaked pie shell, and set aside.

To make the meringue, combine the sugar and water in a saucepan; cook over high heat, stirring, 3 to 5 minutes, until a syrup forms and the temperature reads 200°F on a candy thermometer. Remove it from heat; set aside. Beat whites until foamy; add cream of tartar; continue beating about 3 more minutes, until whites form stiff peaks. Continue to beat, and carefully drizzle syrup into whites until meringue is smooth and shiny.

Using a rubber spatula, cover the filling with meringue and return tart to oven 10 to 15 minutes, until the meringue is browned. Cool tart on a rack and refrigerate at least 4 hours before serving.

MAKES 10 SERVINGS

Cherry Crisp à la Mode

Just as the name implies, a perfect cherry crisp is a delicious layer of sweet and bubbly fruit covered by a crisp, crumbly sweet topping. There's really no better way to serve such a dish except à la mode.

1	POUND CHERRIES, STEMMED AND PITTED	¼	CUP WHOLE-WHEAT FLOUR
1	CUP TRANS FATS FREE MARGARINE	1	TEASPOON ALMOND EXTRACT
1¼	CUP RAW UNREFINED SUGAR		NONDAIRY ICE CREAM OR ICE CREAM OF YOUR
¼	CUP UNBLEACHED WHITE FLOUR		CHOICE

Preheat the oven to 350°F. Combine the cherries, ½ cup of the margarine, and ¾ cup of the sugar in a large saucepan. Cook over medium heat until the cherries are soft and tender. Using a slotted spoon, transfer the cherries to a 9-by-13-inch baking dish.

Sift together the flours, the remaining ½ cup sugar, and the almond extract. Using your fingers or a pastry cutter, work the remaining margarine into the dry ingredients until the mixture resembles coarse crumbs. Spread the flour mixture over the cherries and bake for 12 minutes. Serve with a scoop of ice cream.

MAKES 8 SERVINGS

My Favorite Strudel

Granny Smith apples originated in Australia in 1868 and have since become one of the most popular varieties in North America. They're crisp and firm, slightly tart, and hold up well in baking, which is why they're our choice for this strudel. Serve it with a scoop of ice cream or yogurt if you like, although it's equally good on its own. The strudel will keep for four or five days in an airtight container.

½ CUP RAW UNREFINED SUGAR	1 CUP RASPBERRIES
¼ CUP UNBLEACHED WHITE FLOUR	8 OUNCES FROZEN FILO DOUGH, THAWED
½ CUP TRANS FATS FREE MARGARINE	¼ CUP SUNFLOWER OR SAFFLOWER OIL
4 MEDIUM GRANNY SMITH APPLES, PEELED, CORED, AND SLICED ⅛ INCH THICK	3 TABLESPOONS GROUND CINNAMON MIXED WITH 3 TABLESPOONS RAW UNREFINED SUGAR, FOR SPRINKLING

Preheat the oven to 375°F. In a small bowl, combine ¼ cup of the sugar with the flour and mix well. Cut in 3 tablespoons of the margarine until the mixture is crumbly. Combine the remaining 5 tablespoons margarine with the apples, raspberries, and the remaining ¼ cup sugar in a medium bowl and toss well.

Unwrap and unfold the filo dough and cover it with a damp towel so that it doesn't dry out as you work. Lay one sheet on a flat surface and brush it lightly with oil. Lay another sheet on top and brush it with more oil. Continue stacking and oiling the filo until you have a stack of 9 to 11 sheets.

Spread the fruit mixture over the surface of the filo, leaving a 1-inch border all around. Sprinkle the crumb mixture over the fruit. Carefully fold in the 2 short sides of the filo over the fruit and roll up the strudel, starting at the short end nearest you, to form a log. Carefully transfer it, seam side down, to a baking sheet and brush the top surface with a bit more oil. Sprinkle with the cinnamon sugar mixture; bake 25 to 30 minutes, until golden brown on top. Cool to room temperature before serving.

MAKES 10 TO 12 SERVINGS

Almond-Berry Cobbler

What could be better than a berry-rich, juicy cobbler topped with a crunchy, nutty crust? That same cobbler, warm from the oven topped with a scoop of vanilla ice cream! It's a classic, old-fashioned dessert.

FOR THE FILLING

2	CUPS BLACKBERRIES
2	CUPS RASPBERRIES
1	CUP RAW UNREFINED SUGAR
1	CUP TRANS FATS FREE MARGARINE
½	CUP UNBLEACHED WHITE FLOUR

FOR THE CRUST

1	CUP UNBLEACHED WHITE FLOUR
1	CUP RAW UNREFINED SUGAR
1	CUP TRANS FATS FREE MARGARINE
¼	CUP SLICED ALMONDS

Preheat the oven to 350°F.

To make the filling, warm the berries in a 12-inch sauté pan over medium heat. Add the sugar and margarine and continue cooking 5 to 8 minutes, until the sugar and margarine have liquefied and coated the berries. Slowly stir in the flour, being careful not to mash the berries, until the mixture has the consistency of pie filling. Transfer the berry filling to a 9-inch ovenproof glass casserole dish.

To make the crust, combine the flour, sugar, and margarine in a mixing bowl; toss until crumbly. Sprinkle the mixture over the berries and then sprinkle the almonds over the top. Bake the cobbler for 30 minutes. Cool in the pan before serving.

MAKES 12 SERVINGS

WHEN IT'S ABOUT GREAT TASTE AND GOOD HEALTH, IT'S THE BERRIES!

Vibrantly colored, sweet and delicious, all kinds of berries are rich in vitamins A and C, fiber, folic acid, and the antioxidants that can help to prevent cancer, heart disease, and other illnesses.

- Strawberries, in addition to being one of the richest sources of vitamin C, are a great source of fiber.

- Raspberries are also amazingly high in fiber and vitamin C. One cup provides 8 grams of fiber (more than what's in a cup of bran flakes) and over half the Daily Value of vitamin C.

- Blueberries are an intense antioxidant—research confirms blueberries may help prevent cancer and many signs of aging.

Ranch Banana Splits

At the Ranch, kids and cowboys really love it when we serve these for dessert. With so many flavors and toppings to choose from, the possible combinations seem limitless. To be even more outrageous, top your sundae with a dollop of Whipped Tofu Topping (page 238).

4	SCOOPS CHOCOLATE, STRAWBERRY, OR MINT NONDAIRY ICE CREAM OR ICE CREAM OF YOUR CHOICE	½	CUP YUMMY CHOCOLATE GLAZE (PAGE 238)
		½	CUP RASPBERRY-BANANA PUREE (PAGE 240)
2	BANANAS, PEELED, CUT IN HALF CROSSWISE AND THEN LENGTHWISE TO MAKE 8 PIECES	½	CUP CHOPPED WALNUTS
		1	CUP MINCED FRESH PINEAPPLE

Place a scoop of ice cream in each of 4 sundae cups. Put a piece of banana on either side of the ice cream. Top with the sauces, the nuts, and the pineapple. Serve at once.

MAKES 4 SERVINGS

Very Berry Tofu Compote

At the Ranch, we try to find just about any excuse to serve this delicious compote—we recommend pairing it with your favorite ice cream or using it on top of any kind of plain cake. This compote will keep stored in the refrigerator for up to one week in an airtight container.

1	POUND FIRM SILKEN TOFU, DRAINED	⅓	CUP FRESH RASPBERRIES
1	CUP RECONSTITUTED FROZEN APPLE JUICE	⅓	CUP FRESH BLUEBERRIES
3	TEASPOONS BROWN-RICE SYRUP	2	TABLESPOONS RAW UNREFINED SUGAR
1	TEASPOON OLIVE OIL		

Combine the tofu, apple juice, syrup, and oil in the container of a food processor; process 2 to 3 minutes, stirring twice, until smooth. Stir in the berries and sugar until combined. Serve warm or at room temperature.

MAKES 1½ CUPS

Matthew's Mango Kiwi Sorbet

This incredibly fresh-tasting sorbet is so simple and easy to make that you may find it to be the perfect way to enjoy fruit on a hot summer day. Serve it topped with Raspberry-Banana Puree (page 240) or on its own.

3	LARGE MANGOES, PITTED, PEELED, AND DICED	2	TABLESPOONS FRESH LIME JUICE
1	CUP FROZEN ORANGE JUICE CONCENTRATE	2	TABLESPOONS RAW UNREFINED SUGAR
2	BANANAS, SLICED		FRESH MINT LEAVES, FOR GARNISH
2	KIWI, PEELED AND SLICED		

Combine the mangoes, orange juice concentrate, bananas, kiwi, lime juice, and sugar in the container of a food processor; puree until smooth. Pour into a metal baking pan and freeze 4 to 6 hours, or until firm.

Break the sorbet into chunks, return it to the food processor, and puree again until smooth. Refreeze 30 minutes to 1 hour, just until firm. Serve garnished with mint leaves.

MAKES 6 CUPS

Yummy Chocolate Glaze

This lovely chocolate glaze is fantastic with Ranch Banana Splits (page 234), but we also use it as a coating for fresh strawberries and as an icing on birthday cakes. When the mixture is cool to the touch, dip strawberries in it, place them on waxed paper, and refrigerate for two hours before serving. To use as a frosting, chill in the refrigerator until firm, three to four hours, before spreading.

¾	CUP RICE MILK OR ORGANIC MILK
2	TABLESPOONS TRANS FATS FREE MARGARINE
1	9-OUNCE PACKAGE CAROB OR CHOCOLATE CHIPS

Combine the milk and margarine in a small saucepan and heat over medium-low heat, stirring, until the spread melts and is incorporated. Add the chips and continue to heat, stirring constantly, until all the chips have melted and the mixture becomes very shiny and smooth.

MAKES 1 ½ CUPS

Whipped Tofu Topping

Although this whipped topping doesn't taste like its unhealthy supermarket counterpart, it can be used in all the same ways. The kids like to spoon dollops of it on desserts, and we use it to fill and ice cakes. Be sure to let it chill completely until it thickens.

8	OUNCES SOFT TOFU, DRAINED	1	TEASPOON OLIVE OIL
⅔	CUP RAW UNREFINED SUGAR	½	TEASPOON FRESH LEMON JUICE
2	TABLESPOONS HONEY	⅛	TEASPOON SALT
2	TEASPOONS VANILLA EXTRACT		

Combine all the ingredients in the container of a food processor and process until smooth and creamy. Transfer to a bowl and chill until set, 2 to 3 hours.

MAKES 1 SCANT CUP

Banana-Tofu Sauce

Here's another great sauce to serve as a topping over ice cream or cake. Bananas, in addition to being the world's most popular fruit, are also among the healthiest—one reason is that they're loaded with potassium, a mineral the body needs for refueling after an afternoon of hard work in the sun.

½	POUND SILKEN TOFU, DRAINED	3	TEASPOONS BROWN-RICE SYRUP
1	RIPE BANANA, PEELED	3	TEASPOONS RAW UNREFINED SUGAR
¼	CUP RICE MILK OR ORGANIC MILK	2	TEASPOONS VANILLA EXTRACT

Combine all the ingredients in the container of a food processor and process until smooth. Transfer to a bowl, cover, and chill until ready to serve.

MAKES 2 CUPS

Mango-Berry Cream Topping

Try this for a tasty change as a topping on pies, cakes, ice cream, or any other dessert. It's a great way to use any leftover Raspberry-Banana Puree (page 240)—that is, if you should happen to find any left over in the first place.

1	POUND FIRM SILKEN TOFU, DRAINED	1	TEASPOON OLIVE OIL
¼	CUP RASPBERRY-BANANA PUREE (PAGE 240)	¼	CUP PEELED, PITTED, AND DICED MANGO
¼	CUP RAW UNREFINED SUGAR		

Combine all the ingredients except the mango in the container of a food processor and process until smooth. Transfer to a bowl or glass container, stir in the mango, and refrigerate, covered, until ready to serve.

MAKES 2½ CUPS

Raspberry-Banana Puree

In addition to serving this vibrant sauce for breakfast with French toast, it's also a component in other sweet and savory toppings. The bananas lend a nice smooth texture that balances the fruit flavors nicely.

3	CUPS FRESH RASPBERRIES	¼	CUP RAW UNREFINED CANE SUGAR
3	RIPE BANANAS, PEELED AND DICED		DASH OF VANILLA EXTRACT

Combine all the ingredients in the container of a food processor and process until smooth. Chill for 1 hour before serving.

MAKES 3 CUPS

Raspberry-Tofu Cream Topping

Use this creamy topping on Chocolate Bundt Cake (page 216), or Buckin' Bronco Brownies (page 220), on ice cream, or with fruit salad. There are so many more great uses for it—I doubt you'll have trouble finding new ways of your own. This topping will keep indefinitely if stored well covered in a glass container in the refrigerator.

12	OUNCES EXTRA-FIRM SILKEN TOFU, DRAINED	¼	CUP RAW UNREFINED SUGAR OR MAPLE SYRUP
1	CUP FRESH RASPBERRIES, RINSED AND PATTED DRY	1	TABLESPOON EXTRA-VIRGIN OLIVE OIL

Combine all ingredients in a blender and puree until creamy and smooth.

MAKES 3 CUPS

Blood Orange Silk Sauce

Thin-skinned and sweet, blood oranges are known for the dramatic red hue of their juice (cut one open and it's quite obvious how they got their name). In this creamy, sweet, and tangy sauce, they take their rightful place on center stage. This sauce is a particular favorite at the Ranch for serving over ice cream.

	JUICE OF 10 BLOOD ORANGES (APPROXIMATELY 1 CUP)	1	TABLESPOON FRESH LEMON OR LIME JUICE
1	CUP VANILLA SILK SOY YOGURT OR VANILLA YOGURT	½	TABLESPOON VANILLA EXTRACT
½	BANANA	⅛	TEASPOON GROUND CINNAMON

Combine all the ingredients in the container of a food processor and process until smooth. Chill and store in the refrigerator until ready to serve.

MAKES 2 CUPS

Chocolate Banana Shakes

Chocolate and banana make a classic combination. Here we use it to create a thick and sweet shake that's just as delicious as any you've had at the soda shop.

2	CUPS NONDAIRY CHOCOLATE ICE CREAM OR ICE CREAM OF YOUR CHOICE	1	CUP ICE
2	CUPS SLICED BANANA	⅓	CUP GRATED COCONUT
1	CUP RICE MILK OR ORGANIC MILK	½	CUP PUREED RASPBERRY

Combine all the ingredients except the raspberry puree in a blender and blend until smooth and creamy. Pour into glasses and top with the puree.

MAKES 2 TO 4 SERVINGS

PREPARATION TIME: 5 MINUTES

Strawberry Smoothies

Sweet and creamy, blending the flavors of strawberries and chocolate, one of these smoothies is a healthy and filling sweet treat.

4	CUPS NONDAIRY CHOCOLATE ICE CREAM OR DAIRY ICE CREAM	½	CUP SLICED STRAWBERRIES
2	CUPS RICE MILK OR ORGANIC MILK	2	TABLESPOONS HONEY
1	BANANA, PEELED AND SLICED	1	TEASPOON VANILLA EXTRACT
			FRESH FRUIT OF YOUR CHOICE, FOR GARNISH

Combine all the ingredients in a blender and puree until smooth. Pour into glasses and garnish with berries, banana slices, pineapple, or any fruit you prefer.

MAKES 6 SERVINGS

PREPARATION TIME: 5 MINUTES   INFUSING AND CHILLING TIME: APPROXIMATELY 6 HOURS

Peppermint Green Tea

Peppermint is an herb with a strong reputation for aiding digestion—and it's no wonder. This tea is delightfully cooling with a meal or at any time of day.

6	TABLESPOONS GREEN TEA LEAVES	2	TABLESPOONS WHOLE CLOVES
6	TABLESPOONS PEPPERMINT TEA LEAVES	1	TEASPOON COARSELY GRATED ORANGE ZEST
3	TABLESPOONS FRESHLY CHOPPED LEMON MINT	1	TEASPOON COARSELY GRATED LEMON ZEST
		2	QUARTS WATER

Combine the teas, lemon mint, cloves, and zests in a 64-ounce (8-cup) glass jar. Fill the jar with the water, cover, and leave the tea to infuse in direct sunlight for several hours. Strain the tea, transfer the liquid to a clean container, and chill in the refrigerator for 2 hours.

MAKES 2 QUARTS

Underscored page references indicate boxed text. **Boldfaced** page references indicate photographs.